T0040145

FAMILY HOMESTEADING

FAMILY HOMESTEADING

The Ultimate Guide to Self-Sufficiency for the Whole Family

TERI PAGE

Skyhorse Publishing

Copyright © 2018 by Teri Page

All rights reserved. No part of this book may be reproduced in any manner without the express written consent of the publisher, except in the case of brief excerpts in critical reviews or articles. All inquiries should be addressed to Skyhorse Publishing, 307 West 36th Street, 11th Floor, New York, NY 10018.

Skyhorse Publishing books may be purchased in bulk at special discounts for sales promotion, corporate gifts, fund-raising, or educational purposes. Special editions can also be created to specifications. For details, contact the Special Sales Department, Skyhorse Publishing, 307 West 36th Street, 11th Floor, New York, NY 10018 or info@skyhorsepublishing.com.

Skyhorse® and Skyhorse Publishing® are registered trademarks of Skyhorse Publishing, Inc.®, a Delaware corporation.

Visit our website at www.skyhorsepublishing.com.

10 9 8 7 6 5 4 3 2

Library of Congress Cataloging-in-Publication Data is available on file.

Cover design by Abigail Gehring
Cover images by Teri Page

Print ISBN: 978-1-51073-550-7
Ebook ISBN: 978-1-51073-551-4

Printed in China

Contents

FOREWORD

My wife Penny and I procured our first milk cow barely three weeks before she was due to give birth to our second son, Rye. Hindsight being what hindsight is, I now see that this was not excellent timing. But sometimes the heart wants what the heart wants, and no amount of rational thinking can tell it otherwise. Heck, I didn't even know how to properly erect the portable electric fencing necessary to contain our new bovine friend.

By the time you read this, Rye will be fourteen, and Apple, the heifer calf that came to live with us all those years ago, still grazes the pasture below our house. She's retired from daily milking now, but every day I stop to give her a scratch or two. She's got her favorite spots, and I know just where they are. I like how she tilts her head just so when I find the one under her chin.

That this story has a happy ending is due far more to luck than to skill, and that's been true of so many aspects of my family's homesteading journey, which has never been shy on excitement; sometimes, much more excitement than we bargained for, or was welcome. But that's the nature of homesteading, and no more so than when homesteading includes the insatiable curiosity, boundless energy, and (let's be honest) occasionally overwhelming neediness of young children.

It's worth it, of course. In my humble opinion, there is no finer way to raise children than on a homestead; there are no finer lessons than those of honest labor and the gratification of providing for self and family. Teri Page knows this, and that's why her book is such a gem, full of practical ideas and skills, as well as the simple delight that comes of working the land alongside your loved ones. I only wish she'd written it a decade ago, when we were still young(ish) parents with a plot of land, two small children, and way too many projects on our hands. No doubt it would have made our learning curve much easier to navigate.

If you're reading this, it's likely you're still fairly early into your parenting journey. Maybe you're just embarking on your homesteading adventure, or perhaps you've been at it for a while. Maybe it's still in the dream stage. No matter the case, this book is chock-full of projects and profiles that inspire, inform, and most of all, ensure that your homesteading and parenting path is full of laughter and learning. To be sure, there will be missteps. There always are. But thanks to Teri's experience and generosity, there's bound to be a few less.

—Ben Hewitt, author of *Saved*,
The Town That Food Saved, and
coauthor of *The Nourishing Homestead*

INTRODUCTION

My two children were born into homesteading, but my husband and I were not. Instead, as adults, we slowly learned how to grow our own food, take care of farm animals, preserve the harvest, gather herbs for remedies, and make much of what we need by hand. My children, on the other hand, grew up in the garden, barn, and outdoor kitchen of our small, rural homestead, absorbing effortlessly what it has taken us adults decades to master. In our experience, children thrive when they are encouraged to experience the connection to nature that homesteading so naturally facilitates.

On a recent mild winter day, my ten-year-old daughter Ella and I collected clay to make seed balls, seven-year-old Everett helped Brian solder some plumbing fixtures, and each of us kept an eye on a large pot of boiling black walnut sap that we had collected in our woods earlier that day. On any reasonably sunny day, I am likely to find the kids building fairy houses on the earthen mound of our root cellar, gathering wild plants for "potions," or observing the daily drama of our flock of chickens. The homestead is their school, the plants and animals their teachers.

I firmly believe that homesteading is a combination of mindset and skill set, and both can be cultivated with hard work and imagination. It doesn't matter if you live rurally or in the city, have years of experience or are just beginning your to dive into self-sufficiency—sharing homesteading with your entire family is a way to deepen your connection to the earth, to the plants and animals that nourish you, and most importantly, to one another. Homesteading is the daily practice through which we can celebrate the everyday miracles of the natural world and learn to overcome challenges and develop resilience.

In *Family Homesteading*, I share many of the practical and playful ways that we've introduced our children to homesteading. I know that homesteaders are busy people, so I've done my best to share seasonal activities and projects that are not only fun and educational, but also contribute to the real work of a modern homestead. In the springtime, the chapters on gardening and foraging will guide you in starting seeds and foraging a wild edible salad. Midsummer, use the recipes in the fermentation and kitchen chapters to preserve the harvest and enjoy homegrown dishes. When autumn comes around, stock your medicine cabinet with homemade natural remedies that you and your children make together. And in the short days of winter, dive deep into preparedness and get creative with some nature-based crafts.

Homestead Family Profiles in each chapter will not only supplement my own experiences homesteading with children with the insight of other homesteaders from across the United States and Canada, but will also demonstrate the myriad ways families can thrive when they integrate their children into every aspect of their homesteading life.

It is my hope that this book will help your family connect more deeply to the land, to the seasons, and to one another.

Our Homesteading Story

It all started with a basil plant.

In the summer of 1999, I followed my then-boyfriend, now-husband Brian to a sustainability education center in the Willamette Valley of Oregon to join their staff as an organic garden assistant. I had no prior gardening experience aside from planting marigolds and tulips as a child in my suburban Boston front yard, but I was young, enthusiastic, a student of nature and biology, and of course, in love.

As a perk of employment, I was allowed to participate in the weekly gardening seminars offered at the education center, and before long my head was swimming with companion planting ideas, intensive planting spacing, and just the right combination of plants for my very own raised bed (I chose peppers and basil).

I had always loved to eat good food and to cook, but growing food opened my mind to an entirely new way of planning meals—one that started in the garden with what was in season. Surplus garden produce had to be preserved, so water bath canning and dehydration became a part of my new skill set. By the end of the summer, I was absolutely hooked on growing and preserving food and ready to dive deeper.

Brian and I found an adorable creek-side rental on thirty-five acres nearby, and began to excitedly plan and plant our own gardens. With each year, we considered how we could deepen our connection to the earth, sustain ourselves on food that we grew or raised, and preserve more and more food to lessen our dependence on stores. Layer hens were our first livestock addition (of course!), which led to meat goats, broiler chickens, bees, ducks, pigs, and a herd of Alpine dairy goats. Vegetable ferments led to sourdough bread, mead and cider making, and cheese making.

Along the way, Brian and I married and became pregnant with our first child, Ella. Born at home on the winter solstice, Ella's first outings were to the goat shed for morning milking and to the greenhouse to pick winter greens. Our son, Everett, was born three years later. Although we (wisely) cut back on a few homesteading activities—no longer raising pigs and ceasing Brian's Community Supported Bakery—our homesteading life with children was largely the same as before children. We just had to get a bit more creative about how we fit it all in! Strapped to our back in baby carriers, propped in jog strollers, perched on blankets, carried in baskets, our kids accompanied us on virtually all of our homestead chores, becoming a part of our daily homestead life from day one.

Early on, Brian and I realized that we wanted our kids to be given meaningful work from a young age. We hoped that they would acquire skills as children that it had taken us decades as adults to master. So it was very intentionally that we involved the kids in as many chores as possible, giving them responsibility as they grew. This was not always easy;

actually, most of the time it took twice as long to accomplish with the kids what we could do alone, but we kept on, anticipating the long-term rewards of our efforts to homestead with our kids.

When the kids were one and four years old, we began a new chapter of our lives, moving across country to Northeast Missouri and starting an off-the-grid homestead from scratch on raw land. Our life was suddenly like a yearlong camping trip as we slept in a tent, cooked over a propane or wood stove, and lived outdoors. And the kids were with us every step of the way.

Children are amazingly resilient, creative, and intelligent, and the way that they adapted to our new normal was nothing short of amazing. As Brian built our house, our young builders stacked short pieces of wood to make forts. As I created a new garden from scratch, they carried straw and raked manure right alongside me.

Now that the kids are a bit older— seven and ten—I can ask them to feed the chickens, harvest food from the garden, whip up a healthy snack, and help with almost any other task. They don't always want to participate in my homesteading

to-do list—after all, they have their own interests and priorities—but when I share my passion and my excitement for a project, they usually want to join the fun. Homesteading with our children has been a source of deep connection for our family, and a touchstone for a life that is based on the rhythms of nature and the seasons.

CHAPTER ONE: HOMESTEADING WITH KIDS

Although the "why" of homesteading with kids of different ages may stay the same, the "how" looks dramatically different depending on the age of your children. I can very safely say that homesteading with a ten- and seven-year-old feels very different than when we had a three-year-old and an infant! No longer am I pausing to breastfeed every hour, there are no naps to work around, and I don't need to keep dirt out of anyone's mouth! On the flipside, now that they're older, my kids have their own ideas about what is fun, not to mention their own social calendar. This chapter will dive into the different phases of childhood and offer some creative ways to make homesteading with kids of all ages fun.

Homesteading with Babies

If you're a parent of an infant, I applaud you! Parenting young babies is physically, emotionally, and mentally draining, and it can be hard to "kick butt" on your homesteading dream when you're barely getting enough sleep and dealing with piles of dirty diapers. Still, homesteading with babies is not only possible, but also delightful. Some of my favorite memories are from the first year of parenting, when everything was so new and exciting. I loved introducing my daughter to our homestead, and she loved the animals, plants, and the dirt (oh, the mouthful of dirt!).

If you're balancing homesteading and caring for a baby, my suggestions are to 1) invest in a great baby carrier and baby monitor, and 2) take your expectations and plans down a notch. We spent many hours in the garden either carrying Ella or Everett in a wrap or soft backpack (like an Ergo or Tula) or placing them in a bouncy baby seat, or cranking out a few minutes of work while they napped, with the baby monitor close by. We often pushed Everett in a jog stroller for his naps, covering his head with the stroller shade, and then parking the stroller in the garden for an hour while we got planting. There really is nothing like the deadline of a waking baby to motivate you into action! When

it came time to milk the goats, we popped the babies in the backpack (or when they were infants, in a Moses basket) and brought them out into the barn.

However, we did not grow our largest, most productive garden or preserve a year's worth of food the year Ella or Everett were born, and we made decisions to save our sanity, like purchasing pasture-raised pork instead of raising it ourselves, or placing the goats on a once-a-day milking schedule. I recommend seeing where you have a bit of wiggle room to cut back on homesteading goals so you can enjoy the precious few months of infancy.

Homesteading with Toddlers and Preschoolers

Ah, toddlers. They are so delightful and so *busy*. It seems like you can hardly turn your back on a toddler without them running away, climbing a bookshelf, or artfully rearranging the entire shelf of books. This period of parenting can be particularly challenging for homesteaders, because toddlers can cause your attention to be split in many different directions.

Toddlers *love* to help, and it's so wonderful and meaningful to involve them in the productive work of the homestead. From the age of one or two,

toddlers can help in the kitchen with easy tasks like stirring and pouring, in the garden with seed sowing, compost making, and harvesting, in the barn with animal feeding and care (with adult supervision), and around the house working on myriad other projects. The key to making homesteading with toddlers work is to have patience. Slowing down is hard, letting a toddler "help" can be frustrating (I can't count the number of times that my toddler weeded out a perfectly good plant!), but the joy of the experience is worth it. Plant an extra row of seeds and let them join the homesteading fun!

As your little ones hit ages three, four, and five, their capacity to truly assist you increases. My experience sharing homesteading with preschool-age kids was so joyful. They love to carry, help, and do it themselves, and it's easy to set them to a task that they can handle from start to finish with little supervision. The trick is preplanning and having an array of those tasks ready. Some examples are hauling hay or straw, scooping potting soil into pots, watering fruit trees, feeding chickens, dogs or cats, or other small animals, or anything that involves sorting or collecting!

Homesteading with School-Age Kids

As a parent to seven- and ten-year-old children, I am immersed in the magic of homesteading with school-age kids. I love that my kids are old enough to handle certain homesteading tasks on their own, with minimal supervision, and that they are sometimes the drivers behind our homesteading decisions.

For instance, my daughter, Ella, loves birds of all kinds and has a particular affinity for chickens. She is often the one urging us to hatch out a new clutch of chicks, or noticing any problems in our flock. Everett is always happy to run out to the chicken coop to collect the day's eggs and he has a strong interest in understanding how things work and putting together machines. Both kids can cook a basic meal from start to finish, and will occasionally declare a "Kid Kitchen."

Still, homesteading with school-age kids can be challenging, simply because their interests and schoolwork demand

much more time and commitment. As a homesteading family, we have found that as Ella entered her fourth grade homeschool year, we had to cut back on some of our endeavors to focus more on supporting her academics and interests. Even if the kids were attending school elsewhere, we'd still have to balance violin and gymnastic lessons, playdates, and school activities with our homestead life.

My most heartfelt desire is for my kids to grow up with an appreciation and sense of responsibility for the Earth and her creatures, an awareness of how to survive and thrive in any circumstance, and the ability to find balance in work, play, and rest. Homesteading is a fabulous way to convey those lessons, but I want to make sure that my kids are experiencing joy in helping on the homestead. We try to prioritize fun and connection whenever possible, while still teaching the kids that sometimes we simply have to work hard, together, as a family.

Homesteading with Teens

I have not yet had the pleasure of parenting and homesteading with teens, but I have had the opportunity to talk with many homesteading friends about what it is like to share the homesteading lifestyle with older children. Over and over I have heard two common themes. The first is to realize that your teenage children may have interests outside of homesteading. As Amy Dingmann, author of the blog *A Farmish Kind of Life* says, "Homesteading is not 'their thing' . . . they have different plans for their life direction, and that's okay."

Second, it's okay to create a family culture where it's understood that participating in the responsibilities of the homestead is a mandatory activity. As my friend Janet Garman of the blog *Timber Creek Farm* says of her now-grown children, "We respected their activities and schedules, but if they were home, they helped." Of course, it's important to make sure that all members of the family are on board with this plan and that the unique personality of each teen is taken into consideration.

Many of the amazing homesteaders profiled in this book are parents to teenage children, so there are more opportunities to learn about homesteading with teens throughout this book.

A Note About Safety

As someone who has trained as a Wilderness First Responder and lifeguard, and led children on backpacking trips and other outdoor adventures, keeping an eye on safety protocols is something I do fairly naturally. Throughout this book, I'll make suggestions about age-appropriate activities, and how to keep kids safe while homesteading. That said, my suggestions might be too conservative for your family, or too liberal. Only you know your children and your environment. A calm, focused four-year-old may be able to handle whittling with a sharp knife while a very energetic ten-year-old may struggle with sitting still for so long. Make adjustments accordingly, and most importantly, have fun!

CHAPTER TWO: IN THE FAMILY KITCHEN

For me, and for many homesteaders, the path to self-sufficiency began in the kitchen as we sought ways to provide high-quality, nutrient dense, amazing tasting, and affordable whole foods for our family and loved ones. We care about the way food is grown, the way it brings health and wellness to our families, and the way it brings community together. When Brian and I want to show our love and appreciation for our community, more often than not, we share food that we have grown or prepared. Sharing good food with our children and teaching them how to cook their own whole-foods meals is not only a way for us to share our values, but it's also tons of fun!

Cooking with Kids

Our experience is that kids are naturally curious about almost everything that adults are doing, and if you take the time to invite them to participate in what you're working on, they will quickly gain skills and knowledge. This has definitely been the case in our homestead kitchen, where the natural rhythms of our days are guided by the harvesting, gathering, preparing, eating, and preserving of food. Getting kids in the kitchen from an early age is a fabulous way to instill a love of food and food preparation that will benefit kids throughout their lives. My experience has been that kids are also much more likely to try foods that they themselves have prepared. Plus, involving kids in the everyday work of planning and preparing meals not only teaches them the basics of how to cook, but also demonstrates what healthy meal choices look like.

Even from a young age, kids can be present and active in the kitchen. Babies enjoy playing with empty measuring cups, wooden spoons, and mixing bowls. Toddlers can help with mixing, mashing, sprinkling, and cleaning, and, with regular practice, their skills quickly grow. Preschoolers may be able to chop and peel fruits and vegetables, assemble and whisk salad dressings, knead bread, and set and wipe the table. Everett, my seven-year-old, can prepare a few dishes independently such as scrambled eggs on toast and his specialty, Chia Pudding. And Ella, at age ten, is now reading recipes and making quick breads, cookies, tortillas, and a roux with minimal supervision.

Selecting the Right Kitchen Tools for Kids

The right tools will make kids' experience in the kitchen much easier and more gratifying. When Ella was very young—perhaps two years old—we first gave her a kitchen knife. My husband took a wooden-handled butter knife and rounded the tip of the knife using a belt sander. Paired with a kid-size wooden cutting board, this was her early introduction to food preparation. She practiced cutting fruit and other soft foods, and within a few months, was able to make her own fruit salads. Being able to contribute to a meal is very empowering skill for a young child!

We also purchased a few plastic-handled vegetable peelers that you pull toward you, rather than push away. This style of peeler requires less force, and I find them very easy for young kids to use. A few other kid-friendly tools come to mind: Microplane graters for cheese, whisks, stainless steel or other non-breakable bowls for mixing and prepping, small wooden spoons for stirring (Brian handmade ours, but you could also take a wooden spoon from the thrift store, cut off a few inches of handle, and sand it smooth for little hands), and non-breakable measuring spoons and cups.

As they got more comfortable with their kid-size tools, we trained them to use "adult" tools safely, emphasizing that tools are useful, but can be dangerous if not used wisely. From the age of one or two, Everett loved to push the buttons on the blender and food processor. As he worked the buttons, I demonstrated how the machines worked; in a few years, he was capably making smoothies himself. His favorite kitchen tool these days is our Corona grinder, which we use to grind coffee, flour, or meat. Because it has sharp parts, it's a tool that still requires some adult supervision, but he has enjoyed cranking the grinder, taking it apart to clean, and putting it back together.

Meal Planning

Getting kids involved with planning meals goes a long way toward everyone happily eating healthy food. I have to admit that meal planning in general is not my forte—I love cookbooks, cooking, and eating, but the planning piece seems to get lost on me. Still, we have a few family practices that help the kids learn the basics of meal planning. The first is "Kid Kitchen," where they are responsible for planning, preparing, and serving an entire dish or meal. The second is to take walks together through the garden or farmers' market and plan the day's meals based on what is ready to harvest. Similarly, we'll go "food shopping" in the root cellar in the winter months. What I love about this method of meal planning is that we're also teaching them what seasonal, local food truly looks like—lots of stews, root vegetables, and apples in the winter months, plenty of salad greens in the spring, zucchini and tomatoes in the summer, and squash, peppers, and eggplant in the fall!

Kitchen Skills & Safety

If there is a particular skill introduced in a recipe, such as separating egg yolks from whites, we try to teach it as we go; otherwise, our primary focus has been letting the kids dive into cooking safely. At the stovetop, this includes learning how to safely light the stove (ours is propane), to always keep pot handles

turned toward the back of the stove so they don't accidentally get knocked, to use oven mitts to handle hot surfaces, and to stay still whenever anyone else is moving through the kitchen with hot water.

When using kitchen knives, we start with some basic rules: no one walks around with a knife in hand; stand or sit at the proper height for cutting; and always keep the fingers out of the way! Using a "claw" shape with the fingers tucked under helps protect them, as does holding food firmly at the opposite end of where you are cutting. There are many knife techniques, like the rock, or the chop and draw, but honestly, our approach has been to focus on keep the fingers intact! If we are working with particularly firm vegetables like sweet potatoes, or very crisp large apples, we may make the first cut for them and let them proceed with the dicing.

Recently, I've been putting my gourmet chef hat on and practicing *mise en place*, which means to "put in place" everything you need for a dish or meal before you begin to prepare it. This is a great skill to teach kids! It reduces the risk of injury or burns because you don't have to run around the kitchen looking for a missing tool or ingredient. It also teaches kids a very organized and methodical way of working in the kitchen, what ingredients look like, and where they are stored. When I have a bigger kitchen (and maybe a dishwasher), I'm going to buy a set of those adorable little white bowls that you see holding ingredients on cooking shows. Until then, we may chop all vegetables into a stainless steel bowl, measure the liquid ingredients into one measuring cup, and make neat piles of onions on the cutting board to complete our *mise en place*.

Homestead Recipes

The following recipes are simple ones that school-age kids can make with very little supervision, younger kids will find fun, and older kids can adapt and experiment with to make the recipes and techniques work for them. You won't find many fancy ingredients, but I have included a few techniques that are helpful for all homesteading families—canning, dehydrating, and sprouting. You'll find a few more of our favorite homestead recipes in chapters 3 and 4.

Sprouts

I don't know what it is about sprouts, but every time my kids hit the grocery store salad bar, they want piles of them! Sprouts are essentially seeds that have been exposed to moisture and allowed to begin the growing process. They are an excellent food to prepare with young kids because the process of sprouting seeds requires very little other than measuring, rinsing, and waiting.

In the dead of winter when our usual diet is heavy on soups and stews and local greens are few and far between, sprouts are a great way to add crunch to salads and stir-fries. Plus the action of sprouting releases enzymes that make beans and grains more digestible and, in some cases, more nutritious.

To begin, you'll want to source organic seeds that are specifically designated for sprouting. You will find a variety of different types of sprouts, from grains and beans to Brassicas. Some common sprouting seeds include:

- Mung beans
- Alfalfa
- Red clover
- Broccoli
- Lentils
- Chickpeas
- Radish
- Chia
- Sunflower seeds
- Pumpkin seeds
- Mustard
- Arugula

You can sprout seeds singly, or in mixes, but you'll have better sprouting success if you stick to combinations of similarly sized seeds. Some examples: radish, broccoli, and red clover; or sunflower and pumpkin.

To get started with sprouting you'll need a widemouthed quart-size mason jar and a sprouting lid like the one seen in these photos. Alternatively, you can make your own sprouting lid by cutting a piece of window screen or a piece of cheesecloth and laying them under a canning jar ring.

1. Before you begin, make sure you're starting with clean hands and equipment, as less-than-sanitary conditions can lead to bacterial growth. Washing your mason jars and lids with very hot water, or giving them a quick swish with boiling water, will do the trick.
2. Place your sprouting seeds in your mason jar. If you're using smaller seeds like broccoli or radish, use one to two tablespoons. If you're sprouting larger seeds like chickpeas or lentils, use up to ¼ cup.
3. Cover your seeds with one to two cups of filtered water and place your screen lid on the jar, and allow the

seeds to soak overnight or for up to twelve hours.

4. In the morning, drain the water through your sprouting lid. Pour fresh water over the sprouts, swirl to rinse, and drain the rinse water.

5. Place the jar upside down at a slight angle to allow the water to completely drain out and for air to flow in. You can prop the jar upside down in a bowl or dish rack.

6. Repeat the rinsing and draining process two or three times per day, returning the jar of sprouts to the upside-down position each time. Your seeds will begin to swell, and in three to seven days, will sprout green growth! At this point, I like to move my sprouts to a sunny window to allow them to really green up.

7. When your sprouts are ready, rinse them one final time with cool water and store in the refrigerator.

There is really no limit to the number of creative ways that you can enjoy sprouts. Some kid-approved ideas are to add sprouts to salads, wraps, and sandwiches, use them as a topping for soups and stews, or to sauté them in stir-fries. If you have extra, your chickens will love them too!

Making Butter in a Mason Jar

Making butter in a jar is one of the easiest and most satisfying homestead activities that you may do with your children! From as early as five or six years old, my kids have been able to complete the entire process of making butter from start to finish, by themselves. Plus, the taste of fresh homemade butter is so unbelievably good that you'll want to make this recipe again and again. All it takes is cream, water, salt, and some kitchen equipment that you probably have sitting in your cabinet.

Equipment:
    Widemouthed quart-size mason jar and
        lid
    Wire mesh strainer
    Medium stainless steel bowl
    Two wooden spoons or spatulas

Ingredients:
Heavy cream at room temperature (You can start with fresh raw cow's milk cream or purchase heavy cream from the store. If you're using store-bought cream, take care to avoid ultra-pasteurized products.)

Salt to taste

1. Place the room-temperature cream in a mason jar, ideally no more than a third of the way full. This is important because you need to have plenty of airspace for the "butter concussion," or the splashing action that turns cream into butter, to occur.

2. Tightly cap the lid and begin to shake, and shake, and shake some more! This is a great way for kids to get excess energy out (and a great arm-shaping workout for the adults!). After a few minutes of shaking, you will notice the cream start to become heavier and thicken, until it looks very similar to whipped cream. At this point, it is normal for the cream to be much harder to shake, but persevere and continue to shake vigorously!

Ultimately, the buttermilk will separate from the butter in a process called "breaking." You will know when your butter is ready because the granules of butter will rather dramatically separate from the buttermilk. This process can take anywhere from a few minutes to a half hour or so, and will go faster if your cream starts at room temperature.

3. Strain the butter into the small wire mesh strainer, and save the buttermilk for pancake or biscuit making.

4. Rinse your butter under slow flowing cool running water to remove any traces of buttermilk that might cause your butter to go rancid. When you press a spoon against the butter, you will want any liquid that seeps out to be clear; if it is cloudy, continue to rinse out the buttermilk!

5. Add a pinch of salt, and use two wooden spatulas to stir in the salt and press the butter into a solid mass.
6. Store your homemade butter covered in the refrigerator for longer storage, or at room temperature for up to one week.

Orchard to Apple Butter

When we moved to Oregon years ago, we lived in a small creek-side cabin with two mature apple trees in the yard. One of them produced apples that were great for eating fresh or pressing into cider. The other, a Yellow Transparent, had a mild taste and somewhat mealy texture that lent itself to sauce making. So began our annual tradition of making and canning applesauce and apple butter.

These days, on our Missouri homestead, our five-year-old fruit trees are not yet bearing enough fruit to preserve, so we pack the kids and a trailer full of cardboard boxes into the

car and head to a local u-pick orchard to pick apples for storing and eating. The kids are great at shinnying up shorter trees and taste-testing each variety, and while eventually they settle in under the shade of a tree and munch on apples while Brian and I continue picking, we manage to bring home bushels of apples and fun memories.

Back at home, we settle in for a long session of chopping. I like to use a food mill (sometimes known as a "Foley" mill) to turn cooked apples into a skinless, seedless applesauce. To use this method, simply chop apples into quarters, removing any rotten spots or large bruises. You do *not* need to remove the peel, stem, or core, because these will all be removed in the food mill. Place the apple pieces in a large pot with ½ cup to 1 cup of water, and cook over medium heat until the apples are soft. Remove the apples from the heat, and process them in your food mill insert with the smallest hole (the one that will prevent apple seeds from filtering through). You will be left with beautifully smooth applesauce.

In addition to the quart jars of applesauce that we put up, we love to make apple butter. In case you haven't yet experienced apple butter, it is not made of butter at all, but simply applesauce that has been cooked down to a thick, intensely sweet spread. It is one of our kids' favorite pancake and yogurt toppings. Traditionally, apple butter would have been simmered on the stove or over an open fire all day long, stirring continuously to avoid scorching, but if, like me, you don't have time for that method, this recipe will use a slow cooker, which is a hands-off way to get the same delicious results.

Preparing apples by peeling, coring, and cutting into cubes is a fabulous way to practice knife and basic kitchen skills, and kids as young as three or four years old can help with this process. Kids can also be fully invested in the stirring and tasting process of cooking the apple butter down in a slow cooker; supervise the youngest kids, of course.

1. Prepare the apples for the slow cooker by peeling and coring the apples, taking care to remove all skin and seeds, and then cut the apples into one-inch cubes.

2. Place your uncooked apple cubes in your slow cooker and add ¼ to ½ cup water to prevent the apples from burning. Remember that the apples will cook down significantly, so fill your slow cooker to the top with apples! (If you've followed the directions above to make applesauce, you can also bypass the chopping and place your applesauce in the slow

cooker to further cook down to apple butter.)

3. Set your slow cooker on low heat and allow the sauce/apples to cook down for 12–18 hours with the lid off, stirring every so often. For a delicious wake up, prepare a batch of pancake batter, and ask the kids to taste-test the apple butter!

4. If you'd like to can apple butter for longer storage, ladle hot apple butter into presterilized pint mason jars, leaving ½ inch of headspace. Top with sterilized lids and rings, and process in a hot water bath for ten minutes.

Canning at Elevation

Safely canning when you live above 1,000 feet elevation requires adding processing time to water bath canning. Make the following adjustments to the times given in this book:

Altitude, in feet	Additional Processing Time
1,000–3,000	5 minutes
3,001–6,000	10 minutes
6,001–8,000	15 minutes
8,001–10,000	20 minutes

Canning with Kids

Water bath and pressure canning are two of the most oft-used homesteading skills. But are they appropriate for younger kids? This is one of those homesteading situations where you really have to evaluate your kids' abilities and make a decision that feels good to you. Perhaps a good starting point is to make a list of all the steps involved in canning, and then decide which ones feel comfortable to share with kids.

Although my kids are involved with most of the steps leading up to canning—harvesting or picking, peeling, snapping, or chopping, and preparing the food for canning—I tend to ask my kids to leave the kitchen area for the canning process itself. Ella, at age ten, might help with the tasks of filling cans and placing lids, but our kitchen is too small for me to feel comfortable with the kids underfoot while I'm handling jars full of boiling water.

On the other hand, my friend Ann from the blog *A Farm Girl in the Making* feels comfortable with her nine-year-old daughter completing water bath canning and steam canning from start to finish, with guidance throughout the process. "I remind her and question her to see if she remembers the steps to come. I have her read the recipe out loud, share with me what her process is, and if she plans to make an adjustment. I am always in the kitchen working on something else," Ann says.

Field-to-Table Fruit Rolls

When the summer months roll around, there are a few activities that we never miss. One of them is heading to a local u-pick farm to pick farm-fresh strawberries. When my kids were babies, we'd sit them in the path between the rows of strawberries and watch with amusement as they found the best, ripest berries as if by instinct! In their toddler years, they would gleefully eat out of the buckets of strawberries we had just picked! Clearly, u-picking with young kids is not always the most time-efficient

harvest, but I promise that as they hit six or seven years old, there are more berries going *in* the bucket than *out*! And more importantly, berry picking is memory making.

We primarily like to fill our freezer with ripe berries and our pantry with jams and sauces, but occasionally we'll make a special treat like fruit leather. Do you remember Fruit Roll-Ups from your childhood? I loved them as a kid, but as a mom, I want a healthier version of this portable snack.

The recipe below can be used as a jumping-off point for fruit roll creation, but the fun really begins when you start with farm-fresh fruit or even a combination of fruits and vegetables (sneaky!). Try strawberries and cooked beets, sweet potatoes and apple, pumpkin and apple, or kale, blueberries, and blackberries. If you own or can borrow a food dehydrator, it will make the process even simpler, but I will also give instructions on how to make fruit rolls in your home oven.

Ingredients:

4 cups fresh or frozen strawberries—if you're using frozen berries, be sure to thaw them completely and drain the excess liquid

½ cup cooked beets

¼ cup maple syrup or honey

1–2 teaspoons lemon juice

Pinch of salt

1. Heat your oven to 170°F or set your dehydrator to 130–140°F. Because our goal is to dehydrate and not to cook the fruit rolls, you may want to prop the oven door open slightly with a wooden spoon to keep the actual temperature a bit lower than 170°F.

2. Prepare the fruit mixture by placing all ingredients in a blender or food processor and pureeing until smooth.

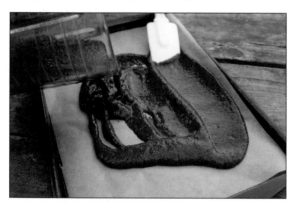

3. Line two baking pans with parchment paper or silicon baking mats, and pour the strawberry mixture onto the lined sheets, spreading evenly with a spatula.

4. Dehydrate or bake until the fruit mixture is firm to the touch, no longer sticky, and peels easily away from the parchment paper/mat. Check on the consistency after four hours, but know that it may take six to eight hours. Remove the fruit rolls from the oven and allow them to cool completely.

5. When cool, cut the fruit into rolls using a pair of scissors, a pizza cutter, or a knife (supervise young kids with this step), and store in an airtight container until ready to eat!

Homestead Family Profile: Corina Sahlin
Marblemount, Washington

Kids ages fifteen, thirteen, and eight

Photo Credits: Corina Sahlin, Marblemount Homestead

Q: How has homesteading with children evolved for you, from the time that
you started, to now?

A: We were so poor when we started! All the money gifted to us for our potluck
wedding in a friend's barn went to building a septic system. We didn't have
money, but we had tons of energy. I remember pruning fruit trees two weeks after
giving birth to our firstborn son, with him strapped to my back. I also yanked out
a lot of blackberry brambles with him attached to my body. The crazy thing is that
he slept through all of the heavy lifting and vigorous movement!

In the beginning, I got so much of my work done while the kids napped.
Homesteading with tiny kids is hard, especially when you are a type A German
workaholic like I am. The kids slowed me way down. Sure, they "helped" when
they got a little older, but when they are still crawling and small, you have to
watch them closely. There were times when my kids pulled up the plants I just
transplanted into the garden after I started them from seeds and babied them
for weeks! They just wanted to help me weed!

I got a lot of work done on the weekends when Steve was home. Most of my
free time was spent catching up on gardening, cheese making, and preserving

food. I look back at those first few years and am amazed how much I got done while homesteading and homeschooling.

Q: How are your children involved in cooking, meal planning, and meal preparation?

A: I cook most of our meals from scratch—with a lot of food we've grown ourselves. Since my kids help grow and pick this food, they are already quite invested in it by the time it reaches the kitchen. For us, meal preparation starts in the soil, transplanting cabbage seedlings, weeding around the lettuce, watering, peas, digging potatoes, and picking tomatoes. My kids know the taste of real food.

My oldest son is a master bread sticks maker; he loves to eat bread and researched until he found a recipe he loves. He also adores sushi and makes it often for the whole family, including a really artistic arrangement and presentation of the food. My middle child is our salad guy. I taught him how to make the kind of salad dressing my German mother makes, and he has expanded on it with his own unique additions. Elderberry syrup in salad dressing, anyone? We once gave him a cookbook for Christmas, and every now and then he picks out a recipe, writes down a shopping list, and then makes the dish. Our littlest one is becoming a cookie-making expert. It helps that she loves eating them, but honestly, she will mix, roll out, and decorate sugar cookies with the best of them.

Q: A common frustration I hear from parents is that they don't have enough time to homestead. How do you make time for family life, work life, *and* homestead life?

A: There is never enough time, is there? However, if something is important enough, you *make* time for it. Growing, harvesting, cooking, and preserving healthy, organic food is a priority in our family, so we make time for it. Both Steve and I believe it's important on so many levels to be connected to nature. Kids aren't supposed to be sedentary and spend hours in front of electronic devices and screens. We are supposed to know where our food comes from. Our children help butcher chickens, and they know what's involved in Sunday night's chicken dinner. It sure didn't come from a plastic-wrapped package in the supermarket freezer. I want our kids to know how to grow, raise, gather, and prepare food, since it is a foundation for good health.

Q: What is your biggest challenge when it comes to homesteading with children?
A: It can be hard to get the kids motivated. It helps to check in with what they like to do. Our middle kid, for example, likes splitting firewood, so we have him concentrate on that. The little one likes harvesting, so she tends to be my helper there. My kids have always been expected to pull their weight by helping. I tell them that if they want to eat, they have to help. They don't get a choice in the matter, and although they grumble sometimes (especially if it's a hot day and they have to dig up potatoes), I don't let them off the hook. We work hard, and we play hard. So once they are done helping, we do fun stuff. We go swimming, hiking, biking, or on other adventures, and they know they have it good!

"I think it's important to realize that homesteading is a lifestyle choice aligned with your values. My husband and I made the choice early on to align with our values: simple, clean, self-sufficient, wholesome living in nature. It takes a lot of knowledge, dedication, and energy to homestead, and if you're not completely committed to that lifestyle and make choices accordingly, you will burn out." —Corina Sahlin, *MarblemountHomestead.blogspot.com*

CHAPTER THREE: FORAGING

Foraging is the act and art of searching for, finding, and harvesting wild foods. Perhaps the most common foraged foods are mushrooms gathered in the woods, but foragers also enjoy wild greens, aquatic and marine plants, nuts, berries, seeds, sap, and more. The beauty of foraging is that edibles can be found almost everywhere, even in urban and suburban areas. Some of the most prolific plants—the ubiquitous dandelion, for instance—have parts that are edible, once you know how to identify them safely.

I'm a huge fan of foraging for a few reasons. First, foraging gets our family outdoors in all seasons, connecting to the natural world and its bounty. Second, foraging fills our bellies for free (or cheap!). Hunting for wild edibles diversifies the palette of flavors we bring to the table and expands upon what we're able to raise in the garden and pasture.

Backyard Foraging and Common Edible Wild Plants

When we moved onto our land in 2013, the first "crops" we were able to harvest were those growing wild on the land. After teaching our kids (then two and five years old) how to safely identify a few edibles, they were able to harvest and share the plants and nuts they had foraged in their new backyard. Wood nettles, black raspberries, autumn olives, and black walnuts were among the treasures they collected from our forest and meadows.

Foraging is an inherently place-based activity, which lends its own joys and challenges. Foraging helps you connect deeply to a particular place, enjoying the wild edibles native to a region, and is a great way to teach kids about bioregionalism, geography, ecology, and climate. But it can also be challenging to share foraging how-tos precisely because foraged foods can be so place-specific.

I recommend finding a local mentor, a foraging group, or a foraging guide that describes the edibles in your region. To get you started, here is a list of common wild edibles from around the United States to kick-start your foraging adventures:

- Prickly pear cactus
- Stinging nettle and wood nettle
- Dandelion
- Chickweed
- Elderberry
- Autumn olive
- Cattails

- Blackberry and raspberry
- American persimmon
- Black walnuts and hickories
- Oaks (acorns)
- Sap from maple, black walnut, and birch trees

Foraging is close cousins with gleaning, which traditionally referred to gathering leftover food after a harvest, but can also refer to harvesting food that is left unused, for example, fruit from fruit trees. In our neighborhood, there are dozens of apple trees that are clearly not being harvested—their fruit is dropping to the ground and left to rot. Gleaners will ask permission from the owner to harvest, perhaps thanking him or her with a jar of jam or a baked good that uses the fruit.

One of my favorite gleaning memories is taking my infant daughter Ella on a backpack walk when we were visiting family in Los Angeles. I was strolling around the dense urban neighborhood, hoping to lull her to sleep, when I stopped in amazement under a huge fig tree that was dropping fruit onto the sidewalk! I picked one up off the ground, brushed it off, and enjoyed the most delicious ripe fig I've ever eaten. Had I not had a baby strapped to my back, I would have walked up to the door and asked the owner if I could shinny up his or her tree to harvest more figs, collecting a few for their own table as well.

Safe and Ethical Foraging

Foraging is one of my favorite ways to connect with nature and the outdoors, and because my kids are almost always up for snacking, going on foraging adventures has been a great incentive for taking hikes in all seasons. As fun as it is, foraging requires a level of attention and care that is important to convey to children of all ages. We have a few rules that help make foraging safe and fun.

1. **Never Eat Anything without Parents Present.** Of course, there may come a time when your children

are so familiar with certain wild plants that this rule can be bent, but it's an important starting point because wild plants and mushrooms can have poisonous lookalikes.

2. **Look for Three Points of Identification.** An easy-to-remember rule of thumb for kids is to look for three points of identification (for instance, leaf shape, flower color, and location). Consulting foraging guidebooks specific to your region is helpful in learning what is safe to eat, but nothing replaces the knowledge of a foraging expert who can travel with you into the field for hands-on learning. Working together as a family to identify foraged foods down to the species is good botanical practice, and good common sense.

3. **Always Have Permission.** Foraging in your own backyard is an amazing place to start, but as your family's curiosity expands, you

most certainly will want to seek out other foraging locations. These can range from a neighbor's property, to a state or municipal park or national forest. However, the bottom line is to make sure you have permission before foraging. Trespassing, of course, is not a good idea, and keep in mind that certain public lands, like wilderness areas, may have a ban on foraging activities (although many public lands do permit noncommercial harvesting of small amounts).

4. **Always Leave Some Behind.** A good rule of thumb is to only forage up to one fifth of any stand of wild plants, leaving some for wildlife, future foragers, and the stand itself. Another guideline is to only harvest what you can reasonably make use of. Sadly, the commercial wild crafting of certain plants—notably ginseng (*Panax quinquefolius*) and goldenseal (*Hydrastis canadensis*)—has caused them to be endangered in the wild. Teaching kids restraint in foraging is a good lesson in conservation of our natural resources.

5. **Choose Locations Carefully.** Many communities spray herbicides along their roadways to keep down brush, and this is a common practice along railroad tracks as well. It's a good idea to teach your children not to harvest wild edibles that are growing in these areas.

Foraged Food Recipes

The following projects will encourage you and your children to get outside and discover the wild edibles in your backyard and region! I'll share a few of my favorite foraged food recipes that bring the fun from the yard, forest, and meadow into the kitchen. We'll also walk through the process of tapping trees for sap to make some homemade syrup. Beyond making amazing dishes, foraged foods can be collected for their medicinal value. You can learn more about the medicinal values of foraged plants in chapter 8.

Autumn Olive Jam

An annual fall tradition in our family is foraging for autumn olives. From late September through October, autumn olive bushes (*Elaeagnus umbellata*) are loaded with ripe fruits that can be turned into jam, fruit leather, sauce, barbecue sauce, and so much more.

Autumn olive is a bit of a misnomer, as *Elaeagnus umbellata* is actually a member of the Oleaster family and originated in Asia. Brought to the United States for soil improvement (*E. umbellata* is one of a few non-legumes to fix nitrogen) and erosion control, among other uses, it is now considered an invasive species. Here in Northeast Missouri, we find autumn olives in pastures, along roadsides, and in other disturbed habitats. In spring, autumn olive flowers burst into bloom, covering the bushes with thousands of creamy white flowers that have a very distinctive, almost cloyingly sweet and strong fragrance.

The flowers become small (pea-size) pinkish-reddish berries that have distinctive silvery spots. Inside each of the thousands of fruits is one seed. Because autumn olive is particularly attractive to birds, you can imagine

how this plant has become an invasive species!

Autumn olive is a forager's delight because there are so many fruits per bush that you can quickly harvest gallons of fruit. However, an important thing to know is that autumn olives are very astringent when unripe and will make your mouth pucker! I don't know how my kids can stuff mouthfuls of not-quite-ripe autumn olive fruits into their mouths when I can barely tolerate the astringency! I prefer to wait until the fruits are fully ripe, when the astringency lessens, the fruity flavor deepens, and I too can eat the fruits by the handful, or cook them into this delicious autumn olive jam.

To collect ripe autumn olives, we like to tie small buckets around our waist, point a fruit-laden branch into the bucket, and gently tease the branch with

our fingers to "strip" the fruits. You may need to pick out a few rogue leaves with this technique, but it is the fastest way to fill your bucket. Last year we were able to pick almost ten gallons of fruit in less than one hour, with three people picking. This made two years' worth of jam for two households! Autumn olive jam is among my kids' favorite recipes, as it mellows out any lingering astringency and tartness and makes a gorgeous bright pink jam.

Ingredients:
  4 gallons of autumn olive fruit
  3–8 cups sugar (sweeten to your
     preferred taste)
  8 teaspoons Pomona's Pectin
  8 teaspoons calcium water (from the
     Pomona's kit)

1. Pick through the berries to remove any leaves, sticks, or bugs, then heat the berries gently over a medium low heat, and simmer until soft. You will begin to see the seeds separate from the flesh, which means that they are ready to run through a food mill.

2. Next, we use a stainless steel food mill (sometimes referred to as a "Foley mill") with the smallest mesh insert, and run the softened fruit through to remove all seeds. This is a great task for kids to help with! Both of my kids love turning the handle on the food mill and watching the pulp spit out the bottom! At this point, you can continue with the directions below to make jam, sweeten the sauce for pancakes, or spread the puree on baking trays lined with parchment paper and dehydrate it into fruit leather.

3. To make autumn olive jam, we like to use Pomona's Pectin, which allows some flexibility in the amount of sugar you add. Combine the autumn olive puree, sugar, pectin, and calcium water according to the direction on the Pomona's package

4. We use a water bath canner to preserve the autumn olive jam for future use. First, you'll need to sterilize half-pint or pint-size mason jars, lids, and rings for canning while heating the autumn olive jam to boiling. Carefully pour the hot jam into jars, leaving a ½ inch headspace. Place lids and rings on jars, and process the jam in a water bath canner for ten minutes. (If you live above 1,000 feet elevation, follow the chart in chapter 2 for additional processing time requirements.)

When the jam cools, you may notice some separation of a more opaque red layer and a translucent pink layer. This is totally normal; we just give the jam a stir before eating.

We love to eat autumn olive jam on toast, of course, but have also found that it makes a great base for spicy barbecue sauces and ketchup. It's also a beautiful gift to give loved ones that may not have the bounty of autumn olives in their backyard.

Persimmon Cake

One of my family's favorite foraged fruits is the American persimmon, *Diospyros virginiana.* This native persimmon grows across much of the Southeast and lower Midwest, and produces small orange globes of fruit on stately trees. They are smaller than the Asian persimmons that you often see sold at natural food stores or in Asian markets, and their flavor is slightly different—perhaps a bit more musky and less sweet; I have heard them described as "pumpkin meets honey."

We start watching a few local trees in late September through early October. Because native persimmons do not ripen all at the same time like some other fruits do, you will likely find a tree that is both loaded with fruit on the branches with perfectly ripe fruit on the ground. Look

for fruits with a dark orange blush and an almost translucent quality. It is easy to tell the fresh fruit from the few-days-old fruit on the ground by the orange (as opposed to brown) tint to their skin.

Local lore and many Internet resources tell us that you should never harvest persimmons until *after* the first frost, but I have not found this to be true. However, to avoid any astringent or chalky flavor, you want to harvest only the ripest and freshest persimmons. You will know they are ripe and ready to eat because the persimmons will be so soft that they almost crack their skin! Because persimmon trees tend to be quite large, the kids pick intact ripe persimmons off the ground, taking care not to squeeze the fruit, as it will turn to mush!

When we're not popping fresh persimmons into our mouths whole, we like to run the persimmon fruit through our stainless steel food mill's largest holes, separating the seeds from the pulp, and creating a beautiful orange persimmon puree. If you toss the

seeds into the compost, watch for baby persimmon trees in the garden! The first year I processed persimmon fruits and composted the seeds, I ended up with hundreds of small trees popping up in all of my raised beds!

We enjoy eating fresh persimmon puree folded into yogurt, added to smoothies, baked into cookies, or mixed into pancake batter. The classic persimmon recipe, however, is a baked or steamed pudding with the consistency of dense custard. While the steamed puddings are delicious, they tend to be very dense, and heavy on spices such as clove, nutmeg, and cinnamon. We were looking for something a bit lighter that highlighted the flavor of the persimmon, and created this moist-textured persimmon cake as a delicious alternative!

Note: If you want to try this with store-bought persimmons, buy the Hachiya variety that is ripe only when the flesh is soft and gooey. The Fuyu variety is eaten when crisp like an apple, and isn't the best choice for this recipe.

Ingredients:

1 stick (8 Tbsp.) butter at room temperature

1⅓ cups sugar

2 large eggs

1½ cups milk

½ teaspoon vanilla extract

2 cups persimmon puree

2 cups flour (we usually make a blend of ½ whole wheat and ½ white, or ½ fresh ground buckwheat and ½ white)

1 teaspoon baking powder

¼ teaspoon baking soda

1 teaspoon salt

1 teaspoon cinnamon

¼ teaspoon nutmeg

1. Heat the oven to 350°F. Grease and flour a 9x13-inch baking dish.
2. Cream together the butter and sugar until fluffy.
3. Add the eggs, milk, vanilla, and persimmon puree, and gently combine until smooth and creamy.
4. In a separate bowl, combine dry ingredients (flour, baking powder, baking soda, salt, cinnamon, and nutmeg).
5. Gradually blend the dry mixture into the persimmon mixture.
6. Spoon into the prepared cake pan and bake for one hour, or until a toothpick inserted into the center comes out clean.
7. Allow the cake to cool slightly, and serve warm or cold. For an extra treat, try it with a side of vanilla ice cream, or a dollop of whipped cream!

Making Syrup in Your Backyard

Did you know that you are able to make syrup from trees growing in your own backyard? It's true! You don't need a lot of acreage and a sugar bush to tap trees and make delicious syrup. Our family taps between twelve and twenty black walnut trees each winter to make three to five quarts of syrup, enough to last our family of four for close to one year!

Tapping is easy, fun, and is a great activity to do with children. Plus homemade syrup is an outstanding natural sweetener to add to baked goods and desserts. Here's how to get started making syrup in your backyard.

Tappable Trees in Your Backyard

Even if you only have one tappable tree in your backyard, it's still worth tapping, even if just to drink the sweet, mineral-rich sap. You'll want to look for mature trees with a diameter of at least twelve to fourteen inches. Some of the tappable species you might find in your backyard are:

- Maples (Sugar, Red, Norway, Silver, Black, Big Leaf)
- Box elder
- Butternut
- Birches (Yellow, Black, Paper, River, Grey)
- Walnut (Black, English)

We like to take regular walks in the woods with the kids and flag tappable trees in summer or fall by tying neon colored plastic flagging tape around the trunk so the trees are easy to find in winter when they have lost their leaves.

Equipment for Tapping

Clean, 5/16-inch spiles, which are small spigots that you tap into the tree to collect sap

A drill with a 5/16-inch drill bit

A hammer to tap in spiles

Food-grade buckets for collecting sap (we have also used clean milk jugs with their tops cut off)

Cheesecloth or a fine mesh strainer for removing particles in your sap

A large pot for boiling down sap and a plan for where you'll boil (on a campfire, over a propane stove, etc.)

Glass mason jars with canning lids and rings, or other appropriate storage containers for the delicious syrup you'll make!

When to Tap

Generally speaking, ideal tapping temperatures are below freezing at night (around 20°F is ideal) and above freezing temperatures during the day (40–50°F). In our area of Northeast Missouri these temperatures are usually achieved in February, but this year we tapped trees in mid-January when we had a few weeks of warm weather. You can always tap a close-by tree if you think conditions are right, and watch to see how much sap flows.

To tap your tree, drill a one and a half inch deep hole at chest height at a slightly upward angle. Use a hammer to very gently tap a spile into the hole. A tree with a diameter at chest height of ten to eighteen inches can generally take one tap, whereas an eighteen-inch diameter tree may hold two taps at maximum. We tap black walnut trees, which are very commercially valuable for their beautiful wood, so we will often tap a bit lower down on the trunk in case we later decide to cut the tree for lumber. Finally, place a sap bucket below your spile so the sap drips into your bucket, and let the collection begin!

Collecting Sap

We do daily sap walks to collect sap, which is a great way to get out in nature and get some fresh air and exercise.

Having a few eager helpers is especially useful when running from tree to tree to check for sap! We usually carry one or two five-gallon buckets, and have the kids pour the sap buckets into the larger buckets for carrying back to the house.

The sap to syrup ratio for a sugar maple is 40:1; black walnuts contain similar amounts of sugar, so you should expect a similar ratio of sap to sugar, but black walnuts generally produce less sap overall. We wait to boil down sap until we have at least a few gallons, so we may keep the sap in a refrigerator overnight until we have enough sap to boil, or we'll just drink the sap fresh. Sap is full of vitamins and minerals, and because it is very lightly and naturally sweet, it makes a great spring drink!

Boiling Sap into Syrup

We boil our sap on an open campfire in our yard. Larger sugaring operations will use specialized evaporators, but we've found that our simple method works great for boiling down small

amounts of sap. You might also try a propane stove, but I'd recommend *not* boiling sap down in your home, as it will generate huge amounts of steam and may leave a very sticky condensation on your walls (as we unfortunately learned by experience!).

We have used a simple canning pot, but found that the boiling-down process proceeds much more quickly when we use a shallower rectangular pot to increase surface area for better evaporation. This year we used a stainless steel "hotel tray," which ended up working quite well. You can find this kind of tray at a commercial kitchen supply store.

This step of the process is always great fun because we end up outside around a large campfire, each taking turns feeding the fire. Gradually, most of the water content in the sap will evaporate and you'll be left with thick, dark brown syrup. You can test for readiness by using a hydrometer, which will measure the density or Brix. We have never tested for density, but simply rely on our taste and smell. The risk with this method is that syrup left with too much water content can ferment. Fortunately, we've never had that happen to our stored syrup.

After boiling down our black walnut syrup, we typically sterilize glass mason jars, make sure the syrup is at least 180°F, pour the syrup into the jars, and top with a clean canning lid and ring. If you feel more comfortable sealing your jars of syrup with a hot water bath, then process the jars for ten minutes. Syrup is best stored in a cool place away from bright light. We have successfully stored homemade syrup for over a year.

Making syrup from your own backyard trees is a fun, rewarding, and delicious process for the entire family, and a great yearly ritual and harbinger of spring. By tapping even just a few trees in your backyard (or maybe your neighbor's backyard) you can make your own all-natural sweetener.

Foraged Salad

Winters in the Midwest can be long and gray, so when the first greens start to emerge from the ground, it is cause for celebration. Edible weeds are among the first greens ready to be harvested from the garden, and I add the fresh, slightly bitter taste of spring to our meals with salads fleshed out with foraged greens such as dandelions, chickweed, and lamb's-quarters, and edible flowers such as violets, redbud, and dandelion petals.

A garden is a great place in which to encourage children to forage because it's relatively easy to patrol the entire garden to make sure that anything growing is indeed safe to eat. Whenever foraging,

be sure to consult a regional field guide and/or consult with experts to ensure that you and your kids are making correct identifications. Kids can then be sent outside with a basket and asked to

bring home a foraged salad for dinner! I currently have the following greens and common weeds in my garden that can be gathered for a foraged salad.

Miner's lettuce (*Claytonia perfoliata*) is a common western spring green that prefers cool, damp conditions. We foraged for this green in Oregon, but because I have not found it in our neighborhood (it does not occur naturally in the Midwest, but some sources say it has naturalized in a few places east of the Rockies); I have also sown it in my garden as an early spring green. Its slightly tangy fresh flavor makes it a kid-approved addition to raw salads.

Dandelion (genus *Taraxacum)* is perhaps the most well-known and easily accessible green to forage. The taste of dandelion greens can be a bit bitter, so my kids prefer to mix it in smaller quantities with other greens.

Chickweed (*Stellaria media)* is widespread in much of North America, Europe, and Asia. It is easy to differentiate from lookalikes by examining the stem; chickweed has fine hairs on only one side of the stem in a single band and on the sepals. Chickweed can also be recognized by its star-shaped white flowers (hence the Latin name *Stellaria*). Although chickweed can compete with grain crops in commercial farming, I like

to encourage it to grow in my garden paths for early spring harvests—in fact, it is one of the few plants that will successfully overwinter without cover in my garden. We also forage for chickweed growing wild along our creek bed.

Wood sorrel (genus *Oxalis*) looks very similar to a shamrock with its three heart-shaped leaves that join at the base of each heart. The taste of wood sorrel is distinctly lemony and sour. Everett especially loves to pop it in his mouth while walking the garden.

Lamb's-quarters (*Chenopodium sp.*) is a common weed in many gardens, and I have several gardening friends who wish that lamb's-quarters did not exist because it can be incredibly prolific, especially if it goes to seed in your garden. Fortunately, this dusty-looking tall weed is delicious raw or cooked as a steamed green, or in soups or stir-fries, so make use of this tasty weed.

Purslane (*Portulaca oleracea*) is one of my favorite edible weeds. In fact, it is one of the rare weeds that I have actually cultivated in my garden, both from wild seeds and also from a golden purslane cultivar. Purslane is a succulent with a mild, crunchy taste and texture. My favorite way to enjoy purslane is in a summer salad along with tomatoes, cucumber, balsamic vinegar, olive oil, and feta cheese.

Acorn Flour Pancakes

Living in oak country, we're always surrounded by acorns, but this year our bur oak tree dropped so many acorns that we tripped over dozens of them the minute we walked out the door. Prompted by our enthusiastic acorn-eating neighbors, all four of us began to fill containers, resulting in two five-gallon buckets of the large nuts. (My neighbor was excitedly eyeing our tree because apparently bur oak and other white oak acorns are among the least bitter, while red oaks have more bitter tasting tannins.)

Acorns can be fine ground into flour, or coarse ground into a polenta-like meal, but first you need to leach out the tannins that make the acorn taste bitter. This can be done in a stream of running water (one online resource recommends using your toilet tank!) or by changing out water every twenty-four hours until the bitter taste is gone. We decided to try the latter approach, which, since it is simply a matter of changing out cold water, is a great project for kids of all ages to tackle!

1. First, find a source of acorns and get collecting! Kids are great helpers for this task; In fact, if you have a toddler who likes to collect, this would be the perfect activity for them. We scurried around the base of our bur oak and collected as many acorns as we could

find, storing them in food-grade plastic buckets for a few months until we were ready to use them.

2. The next step is to remove the outer shell of the acorn. Our neighbors

have a tool designed specifically for this task, which means that they are able to process enough acorns to eat each morning at breakfast. However, most of us lack that kind of specialized tool, so a good nutcracker or hammer will work as well. Winter is a lovely time to sit around a warm fire and crack acorns while chatting about the day. Toasting the acorns first may make the shells easier to remove, but it is not necessary.

If you notice a small, round hole in your acorn, there is likely an accompanying worm inside, and depending on how long the acorn has been stored, the nut is probably unusable. Sadly, we had to toss just as many acorns as we cracked.

3. Next, we ground the acorns into coarse flour. I have read that you can use a blender with a very strong motor for this purpose (a Vitamix, for instance), but we used our trusty metal Corona grinder, which worked perfectly.

4. Now it's time to use water to cold leach out the bitter tannins in the acorns. Place your acorn meal into a large glass mason jar, filling it no more than halfway, and top the jar off with water. Cover the jar, give it a shake, and then place it in the refrigerator, basement, or root cellar.

5. After twenty-four hours, carefully pour off the water—which should have turned a bit reddish brown—and refill with fresh clear water. Again, shake and return to the cold storage for another twenty-four hours. Repeat this process for three or four days and then taste the acorn meal. You want to remove all traces of bitterness; if the meal remains bitter and astringent, continue with the rinsing process until the acorn meal is no longer bitter tasting.

6. If you intend to use the acorn meal right away, you can drain the liquid by pouring the acorn meal into a large piece of cheesecloth or a cheese bag, twisting and squeezing to remove as much water as possible from the meal. If you plan to keep the acorn meal and use it at a later time, you will want to dry it, either in an oven at the lowest temperature, or in a food dehydrator at no higher than 150°F, checking after twelve and twenty-four hours.

    Your acorn flour can now be used in a variety of recipes such as the following pancake recipe, which uses wheat flour and acorn flour in equal measure to ensure proper fluffiness. If you substitute acorn flour in a recipe that doesn't require a lot of rise, like polenta or cookies, you can try 100 percent acorn flour.

Ingredients:
1 cup flour
2 teaspoon baking powder
1 teaspoon baking soda
½ teaspoon salt
2 tablespoon sugar
2 eggs
4 tablespoon butter, melted
1½ cups buttermilk
1 cup strained acorn meal

1. Mix the dry ingredients (flour, baking powder, baking soda, salt, and sugar) with a whisk to combine.
2. In a separate bowl, whisk the two eggs, melted butter, and buttermilk. Add the acorn meal and whisk to combine. (Note: I used strained acorn meal in this recipe, which meant that it was still fairly moist. If you are using dried acorn flour, you will need to increase the amount of liquid by adding more buttermilk.)
3. Add the wet ingredients to the dry and stir gently, just to combine.
4. Cook your pancakes on a hot griddle until they are golden brown on both sides, then top them with homemade butter (page 23) and homemade syrup (page 44)!

Wood Nettle "Asparagus"

One of the most delightful wild edibles in our forest is the wood nettle (*Laportea canadensis*). While similar to the more widely known stinging nettle (*Urtica dioica*), my experience is that wood nettles are far superior as steamed and sautéed greens. With their bright green color, and asparagus-like flavor, they taste like the very essence of *spring*. My kids love eating them, which is fabulous because wood nettles are packed with vitamins and minerals.

Foraging for Wood Nettles

Wood nettles like full or partial shade, and are often found in bottomlands or in hardwood forests. Our largest stands are at the lowest point of our forest and nestled among oaks and black walnuts on a north-facing slope. One of the keys to identification, aside from being in the right habitat, is that wood nettles rise up on a tall slender stalk, and have alternate, somewhat oval leaves. They are distinctly different than stinging nettle, which has more narrow, deeply serrated leaves that are arranged in an opposite pattern on their stem.

Picking young wood nettles is easy—simply cut or break the nettle stalk with bare hands—but as they mature, their sting intensifies, so gloves are definitely called for! If the kids and I are out foraging together, I'll often hold the stem with a gloved hand and ask them to cut the nettle with a small pair of scissors.

How to Eat Wood Nettles

In mid-spring, we like to take daily walks to hunt for wood nettles (or morels, whichever we find first!). We enjoy eating them in the following ways:

- Sauté the tops much like you'd cook kale, perhaps with a bit of garlic and butter.
- Wood nettles also make a delicious pesto. Simply combine the nettles, olive oil, garlic, and some salt in a food processor, and pulse until finely chopped and combined.
- Wood nettles, like stinging nettles, also make a delicious hot or iced tea.
- My family's favorite way to eat wood nettles is to lightly steam the entire plant and eat it whole, topped with a bit of butter and salt. The young wood nettle stems are tender, and taste similar to asparagus.

Homestead Family Profile: Devon Young
Western Oregon

Kids ages five to eighteen years

Q: What is your biggest challenge when it comes to homesteading with children?
A: Time management is an incredible challenge with an active family. Barn chores before ball games and music programs, running home between track and field events to switch irrigation, leaving family gatherings early to milk the cow—these are all aspects of our life. It takes a lot of discipline and foresight to ensure that all animals are cared for and the homestead tended, while balancing the needs and activities of a large family.

Photo Credit: Devon Young

It is only recently that we have set aside certain days and evenings that are exclusively "family time." This last summer we managed to get a couple friends to look after the homestead so that we could take our first real family vacation in almost ten years. It took a lot of care and planning, but was worth the effort for a time "off the farm" that nobody will soon forget!

Q: How would you recommend teaching kids about foraging?
A: Our youngest two children are especially interested in foraging and spending time in nature. They are becoming quite proficient in plant identification and are always bringing me bits of this and that from the homestead for food and medicine making! When teaching kids about foraging, I strongly encourage a parent to teach the three points of identification. Once kids get in the habit of looking for multiple points of ID, they can become very

proficient little foragers! My kids know to bring their finds back to Dad or me to get a green light before eating. Once a kid homes in on something they love, they will see it everywhere—my youngest can spy a salal bush just about anywhere!

Q: How have your children grown and benefited from homesteading?
A: We wanted our kids to understand what real food is. Food is more than what is in the pantry or fridge. It is the sum total of hard work, dedication, and somebody's proverbial blood, sweat, and tears. Knowing this gives my children a greater respect and appreciation for the things we have and the way we eat.

My children have been taught resilience by homesteading. They are creative problem solvers and go-getters. They've learned that if they want something, that hard work is the path to their desires. We have collectively experienced failures and heartbreaks on the homestead, but have learned that each day is a blessing and a chance to improve on the last.

"My best advice to somebody that desires to homestead with kids is to manage your expectations—both of your kids and yourself. Make time for fun and rest. Don't expect it to be a picturesque, bucolic version of Little House on the Prairie. *There will be struggles and frustration, but so long as you can laugh together at the end of a hard-won battle, it is all worthwhile."* —Devon Young, NittyGrittyLife.com

CHAPTER FOUR: FAMILY-FRIENDLY FERMENTS

Fermented foods are not only delicious and nutritious, but they are also a great way to teach children science, food preservation, culture, and history through hands-on learning. Fermentation is an ancient art of food preservation. Long before there were canning jars, chest freezers, or electric food dehydrators, cultures around the world had methods for fermenting food in order to preserve the harvest and stay healthy.

Many of the foods we eat and enjoy on a regular basis, including my kids' favorites—cheese, yogurt, and chocolate—have undergone the process of fermentation, which is simply the action of living bacteria and yeasts on organic matter. We all know that yeasts and bacteria can spoil food if left unchecked. The art of fermentation involves creating just the right conditions to encourage the growth of just the beneficial bacteria and yeasts.

When my kids were babies, both of them were crazy about sauerkraut, so we made jars and jars of it to make sure they got raw, probiotic vegetables with each meal. Along the way, they became involved in the making of our fermented staples: sourdough bread, lacto-fermented pickles, yogurt, homemade herbal sodas, cheese, kombucha, salami, and more. Fermented foods are foods that you can feel good about giving to children. In addition to containing live cultures that replenish our intestinal flora and fauna, the process of fermentation preserves and sometimes produces vitamins, forms amino acids, and pre-digests food into smaller, more easily digestible parts. Plus, fermented foods taste amazing! Try to imagine a world without the complex, pungent, rich flavors of cheese, salami, or wine (I know, let's not even go there!).

The best way to get kids to eat and enjoy fermented foods is to make ferments at home. Fermentation is a fabulous way to preserve an abundant garden harvest, or you can purchase fruits and vegetables from the store to ferment. Kids love to chop, grate, shred, and stir, so wash your hands and get ready to ferment!

Fermentation Basics

Fermentation can be an extremely complex process—think about the making of an award-winning wine or cheese—or a very simple one—combining salt, water, cucumbers, and spices to make the best pickles you've ever tasted! A quick primer on bacteria and yeast, and how they contribute to the fermentation process: Bacteria are microscopic organisms that are cultured to make food sour tasting (think yogurt, vinegar, or sour pickles). Their digestive process creates carbon dioxide, lactic acid, and acetic acid as by-products, among others. Yeasts are microscopic fungi that are cultivated for alcohol production or when you want gas bubbles, as in leavened bread or carbonated sodas. Their by-products are alcohol, carbon dioxide, amino acids, and organic compounds.

Tools for Home Fermentation

While many different foods can be fermented—dairy, meat, grains, fruits, and vegetables—this chapter will focus on a few easy vegetable ferments, homemade yogurt, and natural herbal sodas. For these ferments, you will need very few supplies that you do not already have in your home kitchen. If you venture into more complex fermentation, like beer making, the list of equipment, and the skills required will go up.

Many home fermenters will utilize stoneware crocks, but we prefer to use glass mason jars of all sizes. I like the fact that I can see into the jar easily to track the progress of the ferment, and because mason jars come in different sizes and shapes, we can transfer them into smaller containers as needed. It's also handy to have some cheesecloth and plastic mason jar lids, and if desired, air locks or glass weights that are designed for fermentation.

Troubleshooting Ferments

Fermentation is not difficult, but because it essentially is the process of letting food "go bad," it can raise a lot of questions about safety or suitability for eating. My response is to always trust your intuition and your senses. Inspect the ferment—does it have an off or putrid smell? Is there colorful mold growing on the surface? In general, a white surface mold is quite harmless—it can be scraped

off and the fermenting continued—but a ferment that has mold that has a strong odor or is colorful should be examined, and possibly tossed.

Involving Kids in Fermentation

Beyond inviting kids to participate in the preparing of fermented foods, one of the most exciting things about fermentation is that there are physical transformations that occur before your eyes! Milk turns creamy and thick when it's cultured into yogurt, bubbles begin to develop and percolate to the top of your sauerkraut or yogurt, and sodas develop fizz. Kids can document these changes in a sketch pad or journal to practice their scientific observation skills.

Vegetable Ferments

These rainbow-colored ferments make it easy for kids (and adults) to "eat the rainbow" while offering the probiotic benefits of lacto-fermented vegetables. My kids will eat their favorite combination (carrots, red and green cabbage) by the scoopful.

Using the two basic techniques that I'll share below, just about any vegetable can be included in these rainbow ferments. I try to group more "firm" vegetables together so the texture remains uniformly crisp—for instance, cauliflower and broccoli florets with large chunks of carrots and garlic cloves. Even younger kids can participate in all steps of this project, from harvesting vegetables or choosing their favorites at the market, to cutting and peeling veggies, stacking them (in rainbow order!) in the mason jars, measuring ingredients, and checking on their ferments each day.

Hot Pink Cabbage Carrot Kraut

This recipe uses vegetables that are self-brining, meaning that when salt is added and the vegetables are pounded or massaged and then left to sit in order to draw out their moisture, a brine is created from the liquid in the vegetables themselves. I like to make sure that this kraut is at least half green cabbage because I find it easiest to draw out the moisture required to create adequate

brine. Otherwise, the amount of vegetables and proportions of cabbage to carrots are up to you.

Ingredients:
 Green cabbage
 Red cabbage
 Carrots
 Sea salt

1. Start with the freshest cabbage and carrots you can find, either from your own garden, a farmers' market, or the supermarket.
2. Slice, grate, or food process your cabbage of choice. I like my sauerkraut on the chunkier side, so I use a knife to coarsely chop the cabbage. Slice the carrots into thin slices, and place all of the vegetables into a large bowl.
3. For every five pounds of grated/sliced vegetables, sprinkle three tablespoons of salt over the top. Adjust ratios of vegetable to salt as necessary.
4. Massage the cabbage, carrot, and salt mixture thoroughly for a few minutes, then let it sit for ten to fifteen minutes so the vegetables can release their natural juices.
5. Pack the veggies tightly in a glass jar or ceramic crock, frequently pounding it down with either your fist or a kraut pounder.
6. Loosely place a lid on the jar or crock, and store on your kitchen counter,

where you can check on it each day. You want to make sure their liquid always covers the vegetables. If the vegetables have not generated enough brine liquid to cover the vegetables completely, you can mix up a quick batch of saltwater brine with one tablespoon of salt in one pint of water and pour it into the mason jar. Some people place a clean rock or glass weight in their jar to keep the cabbage/carrots weighted down.

7. After a few days, you will notice some bubbling. This is a great sign of lacto-fermentation! Each day, sample a bit of your kraut, and when it has fermented to your liking, transfer the jar of kraut to a cool place. I prefer to move my ferments to cool storage on the earlier side, so my sauerkraut remains nice and crisp, which is how my kids like it.

Rainbow Veggie Ferment

When not-quite-so-juicy vegetables are used, or when the vegetables are cut into larger chunks, it is necessary to create a saltwater brine for the lacto-fermentation process. I used cauliflower, carrots, and zucchini for this rainbow ferment, but feel free to get creative! Asparagus, radishes, garlic scapes, broccoli, or jicama would all be great additions. And don't stop at just vegetables! Capture your family's favorite flavors with herbs or spices that will add an extra punch. Some ideas are dill seed, garlic, red pepper flakes, coriander, black peppercorns, or juniper berries.

Ingredients:
Cauliflower
Carrots
Zucchini
Spices or herbs of your choice
Salt
Water

1. Chop your vegetables into equal sized pieces and place them in a widemouthed quart-size mason jar along with any desired spices.

2. Prepare your salt brine by adding two tablespoons salt (I like to use Himalayan red salt or sea salt) to one quart of water and shake to dissolve the salt completely.

3. Add enough brine to completely cover the veggies and spices and loosely cover with a mason jar lid or cloth. Do not tighten the lid.

4. Place your jar on the counter in a spot where you can keep an eye on your ferment. Once a day, make sure the vegetables are still under the salt brine. You may find it helpful to weigh them down with a rock or piece of glass designed for fermentation.

5. After two or three days, do a taste test. The longer the vegetables ferment, the more flavorful and soft they will get. I find that my kids prefer a more mild taste and crisp texture, which would call for a shorter fermentation period.

6. When the veggies have fermented to your liking, move them into cold storage such as the fridge or a root cellar.

Fermented Carrot Sticks

Carrot sticks are a quintessential kid snack, but truth be told, they lack a certain "punch." These lacto-fermented carrot sticks not only have a salty-tangy flavor, but are also packed with probiotics and vitamins. Make a fresh batch every week or so, and keep them front and center in the fridge for when the entire family needs a quick healthy snack.

Carrots are incredibly versatile vegetables so they naturally lend themselves to a number of creative flavor combinations. I like to add any (or all!) of the following to my fermented carrot sticks (although my kids tell me that they did *not* appreciate the addition of cinnamon sticks!): Garlic, dill, cinnamon, jalapeños and cilantro, onion, horseradish, ginger, turmeric.

Ingredients:
Carrots
Spices of choice
Sea salt
Water

1. Prepare the carrots for fermentation by peeling and cutting them into sticks.
2. Prepare the salt brine by adding two tablespoons salt (I like to use Himalayan red salt or sea salt) to one quart of water and shake to dissolve the salt completely.
3. Add desired vegetables, herbs, and spices to widemouthed quart or pint mason jars, and then fill in the remaining space with your carrot sticks.

4. Pour the salt brine over the carrot sticks, ensuring that they are completely covered. You may need to weigh the carrots down with a clean rock or a glass weight designed for fermentation.
5. Place a lid loosely on the jar, and set the jar on the counter, or in another location where you will remember to check on the ferment daily. You will notice bubbles forming after a few days—this is completely normal and desired!
6. Allow your carrot sticks to ferment for two to five days, tasting them along the way (warmer temperatures will cause the fermentation to happen more quickly). When your carrot sticks have fermented to your liking, move them to the refrigerator or another cool location, and enjoy on their own or serve with your favorite dip or the Yogurt Cheese found later this chapter (page 72).

Ginger Bug

A ginger bug is a really cool ferment with a fun name that kids can make with very minimal parent supervision. A ginger bug is essentially a starter culture, much like a sourdough starter is to bread, or a SCOBY is to kombucha. With a ginger bug, you can naturally ferment homemade sodas, ginger ale, root beer, and other healthy soda alternatives.

Using three simple ingredients—organic ginger root, sugar, and water—a ginger bug will "capture" wild yeasts and bacteria that will eat the sugar in the ginger bug and emit carbon dioxide as a "waste" product; hence the ability to give sodas a natural fizz of bubbles. A ginger bug has natural kid-appeal because of its name, and because the process requires "feeding" your ginger bug each day, much like a pet!

Ingredients:

3 tablespoons grated or finely chopped organic ginger root

½ cup sugar

2 cups water

Plus: Additional sugar and organic ginger root for feeding

1. Place the ginger, sugar, and water in a quart-size widemouthed mason jar and shake gently to dissolve the sugar.

2. Cover the jar with cheesecloth or a coffee filter and a lid ring or rubber band and set the jar in a warm spot to ferment.

3. Every day for the next week, add one tablespoon each of finely chopped (or grated) ginger and sugar to "feed" the ginger bug. Toward the end of the week you should notice some bubbly action in the jar.

4. Once bubbles have formed at the top of the ginger bug, it is ready for use in the herbal homemade soda recipe. Strain the amount that you need for the soda recipe, and replenish the ginger bug for future use.

5. To keep the ginger bug alive, feed it daily as above. Or, you can store the ginger bug in a refrigerator and feed it once a week. When you are ready to use it again, place it in a room-temperature location and resume feeding it daily.

Homemade Herbal Soda

We're usually not a soda drinking family, but on a hot, humid summer day, sometimes the most thirst-quenching drink we can imagine is cold, sweet, and fizzy: A soda. Fortunately, it is very easy to make your own delicious, all-natural alternative to store-bought soda at home. We like to make ours infused with herbs and flowers from the garden.

We will use a ginger bug as a starter culture. The bacteria in the ginger bug will "eat" sugar and create a tart flavor during the process of lactic acid fermentation. The action of the yeast carbonates the soda; as they eat a small amount of the sugar, they make carbon dioxide gas, which is trapped in the bottle, builds up pressure, and forms the carbonation.

Making soda is not an exact science. You'll want to get the proportions and timing pretty close to the recipe below, but don't worry if you wiggle on quantities or ingredients. The point is to have fun and be creative! Send the kids out to harvest edible flowers or herbs from the garden and experiment. We have used sage, anise hyssop, and elderflowers and all three have been delicious, but you could also use calendula, chamomile, dandelion petals, rhubarb, lavender, and so on!

Ingredients:

A large handful of herbs or edible flowers of choice

One gallon of water

1½ cups organic sugar (*Or honey or other real sweetener. If you want it sweeter, add up to 2 cups of sugar the next time.*)

4 tablespoons lemon juice

1 cup ginger bug starter

Flip-top glass bottles

1. Place the large handful of herbs in one gallon of water. Bring to a boil, and then allow to steep and cool slightly before adding sugar. Stir to dissolve the sugar completely.
2. When the liquid has cooled to room temperature, stir the lemon juice and ginger bug starter into the "tea." Mix well.

Although the cold slows the activity of the yeast, it doesn't stop it altogether, so plan on drinking it within the week.

6. Open carefully, cracking the seal slowly to monitor how much carbonation has occurred. Sometimes, it may foam out a bit like champagne, so hold the bottle over a bowl to capture any spill. Serve cold, or over ice, and enjoy!

3. Using a funnel for spill-proof pouring and a strainer to catch plant material, pour the soda into bottles. You can use flip-top bottles designed for brewing or food-grade plastic soda bottles.

4. Set the bottles in a room-temperature location for around forty-eight hours (thirty-six in warmer summer weather) to develop carbonation. This is when you need to be most attentive to your soda. *If you leave it in a warm environment for too long, the CO_2 gas pressure can become so great that the bottles can explode, with potentially injurious results.*

5. If you want to check for fizz, you can slightly crack open one of the bottles to see how fizzy it is, then recap it quickly. When the soda is sufficiently carbonated, move the bottles to your refrigerator or another cold location.

Fizzy Fruit Juice Kombucha

Years ago Brian ordered a SCOBY and began making kombucha in our homestead kitchen. I remember trying it and immediately spitting it out—I hated the strong vinegar flavor! Fast-forward a decade and a half and kombucha turns up in our rural Midwest grocery store, but this time with fun flavors like Raspberry Chia. I had to give it another chance. Turns out, not only did I love this sweeter, fizzy kombucha, but so did my kids. I got a SCOBY from a friend and started making kombucha at home (for a fraction of the cost of store-bought!).

If you haven't yet experienced kombucha, it is a fermented beverage made from tea, sugar, and a culture called a SCOBY, or a Symbiotic Culture of Bacteria and Yeast. During the fermentation process, the SCOBY "eats" the sugar and creates a tart, tangy liquid. This initial ferment is quite lovely to drink—its tanginess can be controlled by the length of fermentation—but in my opinion, the real magic happens in the secondary ferment, when a variety of ingredients such as fruit juice, ginger, whole fruit, chia, lemon, and other flavors can be added to accent the kombucha tang and to generate fizz.

Kombucha is also a great way to introduce healthy probiotics into your kids' diet, and kids seem to love (or at least be fascinated by) the mysterious blob-like form of the kombucha SCOBY. It's a great project for measuring and mixing practice, and for coming up with creative secondary ferment combinations. Some of our favorite flavor combinations are:

- Lemon juice and ginger
- Blueberry fruit and vanilla extract
- Strawberry fruit and basil leaves
- Pineapple juice and coconut water
- Elderberry syrup and honey
- Peach fruit and ginger

Ingredients:
½ gallon water
4 teaspoons loose black tea or 2 tea
   bags
½ cup organic sugar
SCOBY with a bit of starter tea
1 cup of fruit juice for the secondary
   ferment

SCOBY starters can be purchased online, or you can ask around in your community or online for a SCOBY. Because the SCOBY multiplies with each batch, regular kombucha makers always have extra SCOBY to go around and are usually happy to spread the SCOBY love!

1. Brew a batch of tea by boiling water and steeping the loose tea leaves or the tea bags. Add the sugar and stir to dissolve completely. Allow

five to seven days. Kombucha will ferment more quickly in warmer temperatures, and as it ferments, it will develop a stronger, sour-tangy flavor.

4. When the kombucha flavor is to your liking, you can either drink it as is, or you can proceed to the secondary ferment!

   For the secondary ferment, you'll need one cup of fruit juice and enough tightly sealing containers (like Grolsch flip-top beer bottles) to hold your kombucha.

5. Remove your SCOBY and a bit of kombucha and place them in a glass jar to start a new batch.

6. Divide your fruit juice equally among your glass bottles and top off the bottle with your kombucha. Seal the lid and place the bottle in a safe place to ferment for two to five days (fermentation will happen more quickly in warmer temperatures). *Important Safety Note: At this stage, the fermentation of the sugary fruit juice will create carbon dioxide, which is what will make your kombucha fizzy. However, the carbon dioxide can also cause your glass jars to explode if the fermentation is left unchecked.* Carefully "burp" your bottle each day to check on the level of carbonation, and store in a safe location, away from children. A cooler is an option we have used in the past.

the sweetened tea to cool to room temperature.

2. Strain the sweetened tea into a large glass mason jar or glass dispenser and add your SCOBY and starter tea. Cover with a piece of breathable cloth (cheesecloth or a lightweight tea towel work well) and secure with a rubber band.

3. Place your kombucha out of direct sunlight in a room-temperature location. Depending on how warm the ambient temperature is, check the flavor of your kombucha in

7. When your kombucha has developed fizz, move it to the refrigerator or drink immediately! If I plan to add chia to my kombucha, I generally do it at this point.

Homemade Yogurt and Yogurt Cheese

When we had a small herd of Jersey cows, yogurt making was a weekly activity and we used a simple method of making yogurt that is easy to replicate at home with creamy, delicious results. Yogurt is a favorite of our kids, and they love it even more when we top a bit of plain yogurt with some home canned peaches, jam, or syrup! Yogurt is also a great addition to many recipes and baked goods; I regularly replace up to half of the amount of butter or oil with yogurt when I'm making quick breads and muffins.

To make yogurt, you'll need milk and a starter culture. Raw, whole milk is ideal, but you can also use store-bought milk, as long as you avoid ultra-pasteurized milk. A starter culture can either be purchased online from a store like Cultures for Health (see Additional Resources) or you can culture with a small container of plain store-bought yogurt. You'll also need a few supplies such as a large pot, a thermometer, and a place to incubate the yogurt at a consistent temperature. Some people use their oven, a food dehydrator, a slow cooker, or a commercial yogurt maker, but we choose to use a low-tech "haybox," otherwise known as a retained-heat cooker. Brian made our haybox, but you can easily replicate one at home with a cooler and some blankets or a sleeping bag.

Kids can participate in many of the steps of making yogurt (and eating, of course), but some of the steps involve high temperatures and hot water, so careful supervision of younger children is necessary.

1. Pour your milk into a large stainless steel pot, and heat over medium heat to 180°F, stirring occasionally.
2. When the milk reaches 180°F turn the heat off and allow the milk to cool to 116°F.
3. Add either your starter culture or a generous two tablespoons of your yogurt starter and mix well, stirring gently with a long-handled spoon or a whisk.

4. Place your yogurt into your incubator of choice. If you're using a haybox, we sometimes like to add a jar of warm

water to keep the yogurt warm. Tuck a blanket around the jar and allow it to incubate overnight, or at least ten to twelve hours at 95–115°F. The flavor of the yogurt will get tangier the longer it is allowed to incubate.

5. If you plan to regularly make yogurt at home, save two to three tablespoons of the yogurt for your next batch, storing it in the refrigerator in a clean mason jar. You may find that after a time, your culture stops "working," in which case you should start over with either some frozen culture or a new container of store-bought yogurt culture.

If you'd like to thicken your yogurt and make a tasty, spreadable yogurt "cheese," you can do so with a cheese sack or with a large clean cotton dishcloth. Pour the desired amount of yogurt into the sack and hang overnight, or place the dishcloth in a strainer to allow whey to drain out into a large bowl. You can use this whey for baking, feed it to chickens, or even use it for a fertilizer in the garden.

Yogurt cheese is tasty on its own or as a spread anywhere you'd use cream cheese. Kids love adding jam to the yogurt cheese for a sweet dip or spread, or you could go savory and add some chopped herbs and garlic for the perfect dip for your fermented carrot sticks!

Homestead Family Profile: Shannon Stonger
Central Texas

Kids ages eleven, nine, six, four, and two

Q: When did you start homesteading, and what made you begin?
A: We moved from Michigan to our off-grid homestead in Texas in October 2011. We began homesteading for many reasons, not the least of which was the ability to spend our days working at something that would allow us to work alongside of our children and pursue those things that are most important to us. In addition, we feel a heavy obligation to feed ourselves, our children, and hopefully our community with nourishing food. The industrial food system has gotten so bad that even when buying organic, you simply can't purchase real food from mineralized soils and regenerative systems without doing it yourself.

Q: Which homesteading chores or tasks do your kids participate in?
A: Our kids do pretty much everything we do. From animal chores to household chores to off-grid laundry, they are in on it. They chop vegetables for fermentation or help with making yogurt or sourdough breads. They love eating all of the foods from my book *Traditionally Fermented Foods*, of course, but they also love the fun science experiment aspect of things always bubbling and brewing on the counter.

The older boys and girl are in on morning and evening chores pretty much every single day. They dig, plant, haul manure, and muck out barn stalls either alongside of us or by themselves. They milk the animals, bring in harvests, and help with off-grid laundry and menial tasks. They help us put up food by cleaning, chopping, and packing jars for canning or fermentation. Most of the time we aren't far from the oldest three and one of us is always with the youngest two.

Q: What is the *why* behind your commitment to homesteading with your kids?
A: It really is mostly about giving them time. You can plant a garden, make bread, wash dishes, and milk animals alongside of your children. And what we have learned is that the absence of modern technologies (i.e., screens and other busy distractions) means their attention span is such that they *want* to do

these things. It just so happens that we can teach them lessons through these processes, and more often than not we learn lessons from our children as well.

I really believe that work is good for children, and not just the work they want to do. Letting children plant a garden, build a shed, or even just take a turn at washing dishes seems to instill in them the reality that life is not always about doing what you want but also that to work with your hands is incredibly fulfilling.

Q: What advice would you give to someone who would like to share homesteading with his or her kids?

A: Be patient. When they are young they want to do everything but they can't without your help and supervision. But at some point they grow a little older and stop needing you quite so much. There is a tipping point where they start milking goats on their own, keep chickens with little supervision, and even plant garden beds . . . though not always in a straight line. Our entire homesteading life shifted when our two oldest boys passed that tipping point. Give them the one thing you can't get back or do over, your time and presence.

"There are no neat and tidy divisions of labor or nine-to-five schedules; when you homestead, your work is your life and your life is your work. Sometimes that means homeschool is spending the entire day preparing for spring planting or putting up a harvest but so long as we keep our priorities straight, the days may be long but things seem to fall into place." —Shannon Stonger, NourishingDays.com

CHAPTER FIVE: GARDENING WITH CHILDREN

Gardening is the area of homesteading that I feel most passionate about, so it has always been a priority of mine to share the joys of digging in the earth and growing food with my children. Gardening with children is really quite wonderful—yes, you might have to redo a few plantings, and some tasks do take a bit longer—but the sense of wonder and connection that develops from a child's relationship with their garden is worth it. Just the other day I asked Everett if he wanted to help me pick a salad. He said that although he didn't want to help pick a salad, he would come with me to "just talk." These moments are so precious and irreplaceable.

Gardening teaches children valuable self-sufficiency skills, gets kids outdoors, instills a love of whole foods, and brings the family together in an activity that is fun and rewarding. A garden can be as small as a few plants growing on a windowsill, or as large as your imagination and space allows. If you don't have access to growing space, consider looking into community gardens in your area. Another option for landless gardeners is to volunteer to work on someone else's garden in exchange for a bed or two or a share of the harvest. There are so many creative ways to dig into the earth, and share the joy of growing with kids.

In this chapter, we'll talk about how to make gardening kid-friendly by knowing how to choose the right vegetables and fruits to plant, selecting the right tools for small hands, and creating fun gardening spaces. There will be a few bigger building projects to explore and create together, and some simpler projects that kids can tackle on their own.

Ways to Make Gardening Kid-Friendly

Both Ella and Everett love spending time in the garden because it is a beautiful and magical place. And although they are deeply dedicated to their own garden bed, as they've gotten a bit older, and cultivated their own interests, they are less likely to volunteer for garden work. As with any homesteading activity, there is a blend of involving kids because they are integral members of the family and contributors to the work of the homestead, and also an awareness that they are way more likely to join in the work of the garden when it is perceived as a fun and connecting activity.

Here are some of my best tips for gardening with children, from many, many hours spent in the garden with Ella and Everett.

Start Now

Because I was an avid gardener long before I became a parent, my kids have been in the garden almost literally from day one, but it is never too late to share gardening with children of any age! If you are parenting babies or toddlers, bring them into the garden and integrate them into your workflow. When my kids were babies, they were either on our back in a wrap or soft backpack, or they were on a blanket with a few toys. We took frequent breaks to interact and play, and they enjoyed the fresh air and sunshine! One of the best garden projects we ever undertook was to replace a raised bed in our high tunnel with a sandbox. The kids were totally content to play in the sand while we worked in the garden. We also set up water tables, which were basically non-breakable containers of many sizes and shapes that were filled with water. Pouring water back and forth between containers can entertain a toddler for a long time, certainly long enough to plant a bed or harvest the day's meal.

Family Homesteading

Invite Their Help

Kids love to help, and involving children in meaningful work such as gardening teaches them that they are an integral part of your family's work. They learn valuable skills, and feel a lot of pride. Older kids can be offered more responsibility; perhaps they can be in charge of inventorying the seed collection, flipping through seed catalogs, and making lists of seeds to order, or maybe they can plant an entire section of the garden on their own.

Use Child-Size Tools

For older children, standard adult-size garden tools will work just fine, but younger kids need smaller tools that are not toys. Plastic shovels and trowels simply don't hold up to the demands of gardening, and will leave your kids frustrated.

Instead, invest in nicer-quality kid-size gardening tools with wooden handles and metal implements. When my kids were two and five years old, I purchased some great tools from a Montessori supply company. A reasonably priced set came with a child-size shovel, rake, hoe, and leaf rake. They have held up really well, and the kids have a much better experience using tools that fit their hands and bodies.

Involve Kids in the Harvest

Harvesting is one of the most fun aspects of gardening, for adults and children alike. Our tradition, that started when Ella and Everett were very young, is to head out into the garden each morning after breakfast with harvesting baskets. Even at the age of two or three, I could count on the kids' help picking whatever was ripe and placing it carefully into their harvesting basket.

Of course you want your kids to harvest vegetables and fruit when they are ripe and ready to be harvested. When my kids were younger, I found that instead of using words like "big" and "small," it helped to use more descriptive language. For instance, instead of saying, "harvest zucchini before it gets too big." I might say, "harvest zucchini when it's the size of your arm, from your elbow to your fingertips." This gives kids a very concrete way to know exactly when a vegetable is ready to be picked.

Now that my kids are older, I depend on their help when it comes time to bring in larger harvests like sweet potatoes, garlic, and potatoes. Fortunately, digging for potatoes and sweet potatoes is a bit like hunting for treasures, and they are more than eager to assist!

Connect Gardening to Meals

Because gardening with children is a part of our daily life, and the kids are active participants in the planning, growing, and harvesting of our garden, it's not a big leap to *eating* the produce from our garden. In fact, I credit having a garden with having kids who will eat almost any vegetable— it's just *what we do* in our family.

Our daily gardening walk is still the basis for many meal plans. Usually, the kids are the ones who are totally aware of what needs to be harvested, and often make meal suggestions based on what is growing in their garden beds, or already in their harvesting basket. This is a great way to initiate a lifetime of smart, seasonal meal planning with vegetables.

Give Them Their Own Garden Space

Consider giving your kids their very own garden space, whether that is a bed of their own, a row, or a few containers. Help them decide what to plant, sow seeds or pick out plants at a garden center, and harvest the bounty that grows from their lovingly tended plants. I'm often surprised at how much ownership my kids take in their garden bed. Even if they've lost interest in *my* beds, they still check on their beds each day, expressing great pride at each harvest.

Keep It Fun!

This might be the most important tip to remember. Cultivating a lifelong love of growing food begins with creating positive experiences for children. Know that kids will not always see gardening as being quite as fun as you think it is! Let them water the garden with a small watering can or a hose. Create a big sunflower fort or green bean teepee. Make fairy houses amid the rhubarb. Share laughter and love in the garden.

Garden Planning

Although Ella and Everett contribute to the entire family garden, they each have their own garden bed that they are responsible for planning and planting. Each year they seem to have very specific ideas about what they'd like to plant (Ella's plan usually involves melons and Everett will always opt for okra!). I offer a bit of guidance about what may or may not grow well given the space and timing requirements, but otherwise, I try to let them lead the way.

We live in a climate where we can grow multiple crops through succession planting. If this is true for you too, you can double or triple the amount grown in the same garden bed. For instance, Ella may plant spring peas that are direct sown in March and harvested in May–June. The bed might be fallow for one month, and then she could plant a fall crop of carrots and beets sown in August. Everett may plant spring potatoes in mid-March, harvest them in June, put in his crop of

okra for summer eating, and then tuck a fall planting of garlic in the same bed in late September. Working with succession planting keeps gardening interesting and fun for kids, and increases their harvest.

To keep these layers of planting organized, we like to pull out colored pencils and paper and make maps of our garden plans. This kind of visual representation is really useful for mapping out the entire garden, plus it's a fun all-family activity. And if you live in a climate where gardening ceases in the winter months, garden planning can keep the magic of growing food alive for everyone through the cold days and long nights.

Next comes my favorite part of the gardening process: seed shopping! In the

early winter, write or call your favorite seed companies and request a paper copy of their catalog. Catalogs are a great way to get kids excited about seed starting because the photos of the flowers and veggies are so beautiful! A few of my favorite heirloom and organic seed companies are Territorial Seed Company, Baker Creek Heirloom Seeds, Adaptive Seeds, and High Mowing Seeds.

When the catalogs arrive, the kids and I like to sit down with our storage container full of seeds, a paper and pencil to make lists, and seed catalogs spread all around us. After taking a brief inventory of what seeds we need, we flip through the pages of each catalog and make our wish lists. I try to get at least one new variety that the kids are really excited about; recent examples are Dragon's Egg Cucumbers and Tennessee Dancing Gourds. Keep in mind your family's meal preferences as you select seeds. Rather than focusing on plants that are quick growing, such as radishes (which my kids dislike), we'll try to pick vegetable and fruit varieties that we'll actually eat, herbs that we commonly use, and flowers that bring us joy.

Once the seeds are ordered and the garden plan has been loosely sketched out, it's time to get to work! The projects in this chapter will walk through the basic steps of starting seeds and creating gardens that not only produce bountiful harvests, but also are magical to spend time in.

Starting Seeds

Starting seeds is one of the more magical acts of homesteading. From a tiny, seemingly inert capsule comes a sprout, and then leaves, possibly flowers, and food. Kids love to be a part of the process of starting seeds and growing seedlings, and it's a great way to cultivate a lifetime love of growing food.

Because I like to get a head start on the gardening season, I start most of my spring and summer seeds indoors and then transplant them out into the garden bed when they are ready, while my fall crops and some of my summer crops are sowed directly into the garden. Either of these methods is fabulous to share with children, and each has their pros and cons. Starting seeds indoors often allows for early harvests and enables you to head into the gardening season with plants that are already a few inches tall. On the other hand, it is difficult to grow sturdy, vigorous seedlings without sufficient full-spectrum indoor lighting. Direct sowing means waiting until the temperature of the soil is appropriate for germination, but seedlings tend to be quite vigorous because they are growing under the full strength light of the sun.

You can start seedlings in any type of container that allows for drainage and space for the plants' roots to grow. Some options that are fun for kids are:

- Eggshells
- Cardboard egg cartons
- Pint-size milk or cream containers with their tops cut off
- Newspapers rolled into tubes (see sidebar for instructions)
- Yogurt containers
- Plastic drinking cups
- Rectangular plastic salad green containers

With the exception of the newspaper tubes, each of these will require a hole poked in the bottom of the container for proper drainage. You will also want to place your pots in or on something that can catch any excess water that drains out. A rimmed cookie sheet, lasagna pan, plastic cafeteria tray, or garden tray work well.

Soil blends for starting seeds can be purchased at home and garden stores, or you can make them yourself at home by combining four parts screened (sifted) compost, two parts coconut coir or peat moss, one part vermiculite, and one part perlite. Because I like to batch seed starting so the kids and I can work together, we'll typically get all of our pots

ready, our seeds lined up and labels made, and then premoisten the quantity of potting soil that we'll need.

If we're starting seeds outdoors, I'll usually prepare the bed by lightly forking it with a digging fork, then we will spread some compost, manure, and/or soil amendments, which will be lightly turned into the soil before the kids map out rows or grids. Now we're ready to start sowing some seeds!

Seed packets will generally tell you how deep to plant seeds, and how far apart they should be spaced. I also like to keep the seed catalogs at hand in case I need more information about cultivation. When sowing seeds with kids, be aware of the size of your child's fingers. It may be more challenging for tiny fingers to grasp individual seeds that are very small (carrots come to mind, as they are even challenging for me to plant!). Larger seeds like beans, squash, peas, beets, corn, melons, and certain flower seeds may be the best choices for little ones.

Seeds need to be kept moist, but not overly damp because too-wet conditions can cause excess fungal growth that can kill seedlings. For direct sowing, I like to keep an eye on the weather and coordinate my seed starting with a few days of light spring rain. The perfect weather would be a light soaking rain in the morning, followed by a few hours of sunlight! If the forecast is otherwise, I make sure to keep the newly sown beds watered with a hose or watering can.

If I'm starting seeds indoors, we use either a mister bottle or a small (kid-size) watering can, and check on moisture levels each day. We might place a clear plastic lid over the seeds or cover them with plastic film until they germinate, but as soon as we notice sprouts, we remove the plastic. Indoor seed starting requires close attention to light and warmth. I place my seedlings in south-facing windows, but remove them from the sills if we are expecting a frosty night. If starting seeds indoors is something you plan to do regularly, you may want to consider investing in grow lights and a timer. Set the timer for fourteen to sixteen hours, adjust the lights according to the instructions, and keep a close eye on watering; your efforts will be rewarded with more sturdy plants.

Newspaper Pots for Seed Starting

Newspapers rolled into tubes make great biodegradable seed starting pots, with only a few supplies that you probably already have lying around at home—a stack of newspapers, a small can (a six-ounce tomato paste can or any ten-ounce can will work well), and a pair of scissors. When you're ready to plant your seedlings, you can place the entire newspaper tube in the ground, or gently peel away the newspaper before planting.

1. Cut newspapers lengthwise into thirds for six-ounce cans, or halves for ten-ounce cans.
2. Lay your can on the newspaper with an inch of newspaper remaining on the edge.
3. Loosely roll the newspaper around the can until it is completely wrapped. Then fold the bottom edges in, working your way around the can. There may be a small hole in the center, but that's okay as it will provide drainage.
4. Carefully slide the can out from the newspaper roll and if you'd like, fold the top edge of the tube in to create a more stable opening.

Now your pots are ready to use! Line them up inside a deep-dish tray, like a lasagna pan, and fill with moistened soil before sowing seeds.

DIY Seed Balls

One spring we received seed balls (or seed "bombs" as they are sometimes called) as a gift, and the kids were captivated by the idea of tossing a ball of clay and waiting for sprouts to emerge. Seed balls are made by tucking seeds inside a ball of compost and clay. The ball shape makes them easy to toss and the clay protects the seeds until the temperature and moisture levels are just right for germination. This makes them ideal for planting hard-to-reach areas like meadows, creek beds, or forest edges, for gifting, or for tossing into vacant lots or sidewalk cracks, a sort of "guerrilla gardening."

To make seed balls, you'll need some clay, compost or potting soil, and an assortment of seeds. If you're making seed balls for your own backyard and live in an area with clay soil, then you can harvest some clay from the earth. However, if you're gifting these, or if you live in an area with invasive weed issues, you will want to purchase red or white self-hardening clay from a craft or art store to avoid spreading invasive plants. The fun part of making seed balls is coming up with assortments of seeds for different purposes: Native wildflower mixes for a meadow, bee and butterfly-attracting flowers and herbs to support pollinators, or collections of greens for the garden. Help your kids check to make sure that the seeds are appropriate to the climate in which they will be used,

and that the plants are not invasive, and your imagination is the only limit!

1. In a large tub or bowl, combine one part compost or potting soil with two parts clay.
2. Slowly add water, stirring gently to mix without creating clouds of clay dust. You will want the mixture to be workable enough to form balls and hold shape, but not sticky. Kids are great at mixing this with their hands!
3. To add seeds, you have two options. One is to simply sprinkle seeds into the compost/clay mixture, such that each finished ball will have three to eight seeds. Or, you can preform the balls (somewhere in the large marble range is a good size), and then gently poke the seeds in each individual ball. The latter method gives you more control over where the seeds end up.
4. Place the seed balls on a cookie sheet lined with parchment or wax paper, and allow them to air dry at room temperature.

Seed balls are best planted when there is a chance of rain, and when temperatures favor germination. If the seed balls are going into the garden they can be watered by hand; otherwise, let nature do her job and wait for the excitement of sprouting seed balls!

Creating Magical Garden Spaces

Have you ever wandered through a particularly magical garden? Often times these spaces are filled with flowers, tunnels, curving paths, plants growing up trellises, and other multidimensional elements that make you feel like you've been transported to another world. When I see kids wandering through gardens that have been designed with them in mind, their wonder is apparent and contagious. Intentionally creating magical garden spaces for children only heightens their desire to spend time in nature growing food, flowers, and medicine, which, in my opinion, is always a good idea!

Creating a magical garden space is not difficult, and the best part is that kids can be a part of the entire process, from designing to growing. To start, check a few gardening books out of the library (the prettier, the better!) and flip through them together. Which elements capture your imagination? Jot some ideas down, then get out your paper and colored pencils, and working within the space and layout that you have available, begin to brainstorm your own garden plans.

If you aren't at liberty to dramatically alter your garden space, I still encourage you to think about how gardening can be a more beautiful and sensory experience for children. One easy way to do this is to plant vegetable varieties

that are delicious and fun to grow—large pumpkins, rainbow colored greens, tomatoes with unusual stripes, giant sunflowers. Here are a few ideas:

- "Rainbow Blend" or "Pink Passion" Swiss chard
- "Cinderella" or "Jack Be Little" pumpkin (The latter is a tiny pumpkin that makes a beautiful autumn decoration.)
- "Moon and Stars" watermelon (One of my personal favorites, as it's not only beautiful, but tastes amazing!)
- "Mammoth Grey Stripe" (ten feet tall) or "Short Stuff" (two and a half feet tall) sunflowers
- "Chinese Red Noodle" beans (These beans produce eighteen-inch-long, deep red pods and are great for trellising)
- "Valentine's Day" (a spectrum of pink, red, and purple radishes) or "Watermelon" (white skin with a bright pink flesh) radishes
- "Gold Nugget," "Sungold" (sweet and easy to pop in the mouth!), or "Green Zebra" (chartreuse and green stripes) cherry tomatoes
- "Sensation Mix" cosmos (the bright pink flowers and showy foliage make these feel like fairies planted them!)

Along with planting colorful and unique plant varieties, it's fun to think about how the hardscape of the garden can make

Photo by Isis Loran

for a more magical experience. In our garden, we use cattle panel arches to create trellises for cucumbers, beans, or tomatoes. Because they are anchored into two adjacent garden beds, they also create a tunnel that, in the height of the growing season becomes laden with vegetables and creates a perfect shady nook. We've also used bean "teepees" to trellis green beans. By setting poles around in such a fashion that there is a space large enough to crawl into, these

bean trellises become secret hideouts for kids!

I also love the idea of planting a fairy garden. Think about setting aside a corner of your gardening space to grow teeny-tiny plants that can become habitat for a world of fairies, elves, and other magical creatures. Grow ground covers such as thyme and chamomile that emit a sweet scent each time they are walked on by barefoot children. Plant small flowers like pansies, violas, chives, and borage,

Photo by Maya Wells

or grow small greens and veggies like radishes, lettuce, and spinach. Underneath this canopy of plants, place a few special objects such as beautiful rocks, crystals, glass beads, or even the occasional animal or fairy for a truly magical nook.

Composting 101

Compost is known as "black gold" to gardeners because it is the nutrient-rich stuff that delivers nutrients to plants, increases soil tilth and improves soil structure, and produces vigorous plants that are less susceptible to disease. Composting is also a great way to reduce waste at home—food scraps, lawn trimmings, coffee grounds, and other "trash" can go right into the compost bin, where the natural process of decay is accelerated as microorganisms such as bacteria and fungi and insects like worms, mites, ants, and beetles decompose organic matter, turning it into rich soil-like fertilizer.

Kids can be involved in the process of composting as soon as they are able to place food into a bucket. Composting is part of a larger earth-care effort, returning nutrients to the soil rather than overstuffing landfills, but it's also an extremely practical part of homesteading. I would encourage anyone to get started composting, even if you don't have a garden of your own. Compost can be added to houseplants or potted herbs, and finished compost is a fabulous gift to bring to a gardening friend!

If you live in the city, you may already have access to a municipal composting program that whisks away your food scraps and turns them into compost for farmers and gardeners, or you may want to experiment with worm composting. If you have a backyard, consider carving out a corner for composting. You may wish to enclose compost in a four-sided structure, or purchase a compost tumbler at a home or garden store to reduce the risk of attracting wild animals into your compost. We keep our compost pile within our garden fence, and for ease of turning, I like to build a heap in the open, rather than contain it with wood or wire. Any method is fine, as long as it works for you, but the most successful compost piles will be at least three feet on all sides to build up enough heat for sufficient decomposition.

In our kitchen, we go through a lot of food scraps, so rather than keeping a cute compost bucket on the kitchen counter, we keep a five-gallon bucket under our island workspace. Every few days we bring the compost bucket out to the pile, covering it with straw, manure, or leaves (more on that in a minute). The kids know that all peels, rinds, and skin go into the compost bucket so they are naturally a part of the everyday work of creating compost on our homestead. We also have a chicken bucket for chicken scraps that mostly contains plate scrapings and leafy greens.

In the garden, the process of creating compost is, at its most basic, quite simple: Create a balance of "green" materials that are high in nitrogen (food scraps, coffee grounds, manure, fresh grass clippings) and "brown" materials that are high in carbon (leaves, straw, dried garden debris or dried grass).

Avoid fatty or oily foods, pernicious weeds, diseased plants, and chemical-laden grass clippings. The ideal ratio of carbon to nitrogen is around twenty-five to one for rapid decomposition; much more carbon and your pile will still decay, but slowly.

Ready to make compost? The first step is to have your raw materials at hand for easy layering. I like to keep piles of straw, manure, animal bedding, and leaves at the ready and layer them with food scraps and grass clippings. If you've ever made lasagna with your kids, creating a compost pile is very similar—you want to create thin layers of materials, moistening them as you go. I first learned how to compost when I was an apprentice at a sustainable living skills center, where I learned that solid corners are the key to a good compost pile, and to focus on a square shape rather than a pyramid.

I like to start my heaps on bare ground, and use larger garden debris as the first layer—think sunflower stalks or okra stems. I crisscross these to make a square lattice that allows for air circulation and creates a stable base. Next comes a bulky layer of straw, hay, garden debris, food scraps, and/or animal bedding. Try to approximate that twenty-five to one ratio of carbon to nitrogen. Next comes a thin layer of manure or nitrogenous materials like grass clippings or coffee grounds.

Finally, I like to give my compost a sprinkle of either topsoil or fully decomposed compost to "kick-start" decomposition. Once your initial layers have been laid, give the entire pile a nice sprinkle of water to create even moisture layers throughout. Repeat until your pile is at least three feet tall, but remember that compost shrinks as it decomposes, so a six-foot heap is even better!

Kids can participate in the process of building the compost pile by loading it up with buckets of food scraps, armfuls of straw, or small shovelfuls of manure. And of course, the most fun task of all—sprinkling the pile with water—can be done by even the youngest of helpers.

After a week or so, head out to your compost pile together to feel the heat that generates during the process of decay. High temperatures, in the range of 110–160°F are optimal for quick decomposition. To keep rapid decay on track, you will also want to turn your pile once or twice, which can be a labor-intensive process, and one I've yet to convince my young kids to tackle! My typical composting schedule is to make a huge pile in the spring when we muck out the deep litter chicken coop bedding and spring grass is abundant, to turn it once, and to use it in the fall garden. If we have ample manure, straw/hay, and garden debris, I will make a second compost pile in the late summer or early fall that will overwinter and be ready for use in the spring.

When your compost is ready, it will feel and look much like dark brown soil. If I plan to use it for starting seeds, I will sift my compost through a mesh screen with half-inch holes. Otherwise, I add it to my garden beds, lightly turn it into the soil, and plant!

Planting Pollinator Gardens

Pollinator gardens are wonderful ways for kids to learn about ecological concepts such as habitat, life cycle, and conservation, and the creation of a pollinator garden is a tangible way to provide nectar, pollen, and habitat to the many creatures that make plant reproduction possible! Pollinators not only include well known honey bees and butterflies, but also countless native bees, moths, hummingbirds, wasps, ants, bats, and more. We can encourage the proliferation of these species by planting gardens with their food and home needs in mind.

When planning your pollinator garden, remember that organic growing practices are recommended; pesticides should be avoided, as many are hazardous for pollinators. An ideal pollinator garden has a mix of native and non-native species, with blooms ranging from early spring through fall. You may want to consult with your local extension service or department of conservation to see which native pollinator attractors they recommend planting. Some common garden herbs and flowers to consider adding to your pollinator garden are:

- Lemon balm
- Mint
- Oregano
- Dandelion
- Sage
- Thyme
- Catmint and catnip
- Sunflowers
- Borage
- Calendula
- Cilantro
- Dill
- Bee balm
- Lavender
- Yarrow
- Sedum
- Anise hyssop

And don't forget about planting for caterpillars too. Although caterpillars can do quite a bit of damage to plants, if you plan ahead to provide habitat by growing more than you need to harvest, you can provide food and home for the caterpillars that will turn into beautiful butterflies. In our garden, we allow dill to self-sow and it does so spectacularly and abundantly! In late summer, the dill plants are covered in black swallowtail caterpillars. Similarly, when our self-sowing cilantro blooms, it is an excellent source of nectar for small native bees. A few years ago, Ella cultivated milkweed seeds as a school project and planted the seedlings in our garden and meadow to encourage monarch caterpillars. We have since successfully raised a few monarch butterflies from the garden patch, which was one of the more satisfying and awe-inspiring nature studies we've ever done.

A pollinator garden can be as large or as small as you have space for, but best practices encourage the planting of clusters of each variety. Your kids may also want to maintain a source of water for pollinators, or create a salt lick for butterflies and bees by mixing a small amount of sea salt into a damp patch of soil.

DIY Worm Farm

Young children love finding worms in the garden. Maybe it's the digging and seeking worm treasure, maybe it's the wriggling, but worms are part of the joy of gardening with children. Wouldn't it be amazing to have an entire bin full of worms? And what if that bin of worms was reducing your food waste and producing one of the richest natural fertilizers available?

Vermicomposting, or composting with worms, is a great way for city dwellers, those with small backyards, or those who just want to generate their own homemade worm castings (worm poop) to turn food scraps into soil amendment. The abundant worms in your bin eat your nutrient-rich food, then digest and excrete castings. As the caretaker, your family gives the worms the right balance of food scraps, bedding, and moisture.

While worm bins can be purchased from home and garden stores, or even via woodcrafters on Etsy.com, simple DIY worm bins can be made with plastic storage bins. Because the only real assembly required with this method is drilling holes in the bin for ventilation, this is a great project for older children to tackle on their own.

The simplest DIY vermicomposting systems are made from a single bin, but a double-bin system makes it easier to harvest the worm castings. Essentially you will be creating two bins that are able to nest one on top of the other. The worms will live in the lower bin, happily eating food scraps and creating nutrient-rich castings until you are ready to harvest the castings. At this point, you will nest the second bin inside the first, and the worms will migrate upward to eat fresh food, leaving the castings in the lower bin to harvest.

Equipment:

Two dark-colored, opaque (not clear) plastic storage bins and lids (the fourteen- or twenty-gallon sizes work well)

A drill and ¼-inch drill bit

Two quart-size yogurt containers, plastic pots, or six to eight feet tall pieces of wood to act as spacers

Shredded newspaper

A spray bottle of water

A handful of homemade compost or soil

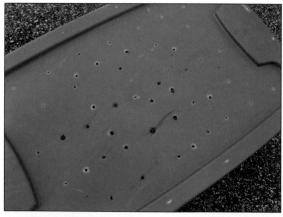

Photo Credit: Amy Stross, TenthAcreFarm.com

1 pound red wiggler worms (see the Additional Resources for suppliers)

Food scraps (vegetables, fruits, eggshells, or coffee grounds)

Bricks

1. Drill ten to fifteen ventilation holes along each side of your bins, a few inches from the top edge, as well as thirty to fifty holes in one of the lids. You will also drill holes in the bottom of both totes to allow for drainage, ventilation, and upward migration of your worms. These holes should be spaced about two inches apart in all directions.

2. Place your empty pots or yogurt containers upside down in opposite corners of your lower bin to act as spacers.

3. Place half of your shredded newspaper in the bottom of one bin and spritz it with water, mixing as you spritz. You want the moisture level of the newspaper to feel like a wet sponge.

4. Sprinkle a handful of your compost or soil on top of the newspaper, and then add your worms.

5. Add one to two cups of food scraps to the bin. Over time, the worms will multiply and you can add larger

Photo Credit: Amy Stross, TenthAcreFarm.com

amounts of food scraps, but to start, you'll want to avoid adding too much food, otherwise the food will rot faster than the worms can eat it.

6. Cover the worms with the remaining half of newspaper, again taking time to moisten it with your spray bottle of water.

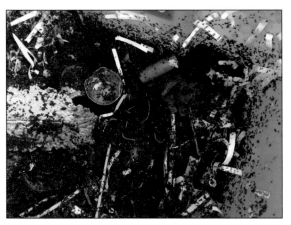

Photo Credit: Amy Stross, TenthAcreFarm.com

7. Cover the bin with the lid that has air holes drilled into it. Place four bricks in the corners of the non-perforated lid, place your bin on the bricks to allow for ventilation, and let your worms begin eating and pooping! If any liquid is generated, it will drip onto the bottom lid; be sure to catch that liquid, or leachate, and dilute it for fertilizer.

8. Each time you add food scraps, check on the moisture levels in your bin. Worms do not like to be wet, but they do need a moist environment in which to live. If necessary, spritz the bedding with a bit of water.

9. After a few months, your lower bin should be filled with castings that are ready to harvest. At this point, you can simply prepare the second bin as you did above, and begin placing your food scraps in the upper bin. The worms will begin to migrate up to eat and you will be able to remove the lower bin, harvest the castings, and clean the bin so it's ready for reuse!

Grow Veggies from Table Scraps

Instead of composting carrot tops, onion bottoms, avocado pits, celery bases, or romaine lettuce hearts, you can save these food scraps and re-grow them. Ella and Everett have successfully grown green onions from bulbs that were sprouting, attempted to grow pineapples, and although we knew that we'd never harvest an avocado from our tree, we had great fun growing two-foot-tall avocado trees from the pits.

Currently, we are re-growing celery. To do so, save the base of the bunch of celery and place it upright in a small bowl of warm water in a sunny location. Change the water every other day, and use a mister to gently spray the entire celery plant every other day. After a week or so, you should begin to see signs of the inner green leaves sprouting from the base. At this point, move the celery base to a container of soil. Continue to water the celery plant well and harvest when the stalks have fully grown! This is a great way to enjoy the fun of growing your own food year-round!

Herb Spirals

Herb spirals are a popular permaculture project that could easily be a whole-family activity. Herb spirals use slate, rock, or brick to build up a three-dimensional garden bed that spirals as it moves vertically. The result is a compact, space efficient way to plant herbs (or other plants). Because herb spirals are visually stunning and full of herbs that are fun to look at, touch, and smell, they are wonderful ways for kids to literally get their hands into herb gardening.

Herb spirals are built by either first creating a mound of soil on a layer of cardboard (to suppress weeds), and then wedging rocks around the mound in a spiral fashion, or by doing it the opposite way—laying out the spiral shape with

rocks first, and then building up the mound of soil. Herb spirals create various microclimates that support the growth of different herbs; for instance, herbs that prefer less full sun, like cilantro, can be planted on the shady side of the spiral, while full-sun-loving plants like basil or rosemary would do well near the top south side of the spiral.

If you decide to create an herb spiral, keep in mind that certain herbs have the tendency to spread, either by seed or underground. Consider planting mints (chocolate mint is a kid favorite) and lemon balm in pots nearby. Also, if you are trying to plant larger quantities of herbs for preserving or using medicinally, the herb spiral may not be enough space. Still, it's a great option for small backyards, or to add visual interest to the garden.

Kids may be excited to help lay out the herb spiral, carry rocks (preschool age kids are especially good at this!), and select and plant herbs. There are so many varieties of herbs to choose from, but consider adding a few interesting scents like pineapple sage, or lemon basil. Add a few bright-colored, multiuse, edible flowers such as calendula, borage, or nasturtium, and let the kids explore the herb garden with all of their senses!

Growing Giant Pumpkins

If you've ever been to a state or county fair, you may have seen giant record-setting pumpkins weighing in at over one thousand pounds! While your family's homestead goals may not include vying for the title of champion pumpkin grower, growing an enormous pumpkin or two would be a fun way to connect in the garden.

Giant pumpkins begin with the right seed; the Dill's Atlantic Giant Pumpkin routinely weighs in at over four hundred to five hundred pounds! Pumpkins require rich, fertile, preferably loamy soil and full sun, so prepare your pumpkin patch with at least six inches of composted manure or compost. If you live in an area with a short growing season, you may want to consider starting your pumpkin seeds indoors and transplanting the most vigorous seedlings under a cold frame or cloche. Pumpkins will grow best with consistent,

Photo by Isis Loran

adequate moisture such that the soil is evenly moist, but not soggy, so you may need to supplement with hand watering, or drip irrigation.

Usually, if I'm growing pumpkins or winter squash, I don't worry about removing flowers until the end of the summer is growing near, at which time I remove any new blooms so the vine can put all of its energy into maturing fruit. To grow a giant pumpkin, however, remove all flowers until the vine has reached nine or ten feet in length. Allow several fruits to develop, but then select only the largest and remove all subsequent flowers. Some growers even prune the side vines to prevent the pumpkin plant from putting too much energy into leafy growth.

Another key to growing giant pumpkins is to provide ample fertility throughout the growing season. During the period of intense leafy growth, nitrogen-rich organic fertilizers such as fish emulsion or manure "tea" can be added; later in the season, to foster fruit growth, add a high potassium fertilizer like greensand. Or, you can do as Almanzo did in the Laura Ingalls Wilder book, *Farmer Boy*, and feed your pumpkin milk! In one of my favorite tales, Almanzo, the nine-year-old farm boy, raises a prizewinning pumpkin by fertilizing with fresh, cream-rich cow's milk. Almanzo's father teaches him to make a small slit on the underside of the vine, near the pumpkin. They set a bowl of milk in a hollow in the ground next to the pumpkin, and then ran a candlewick between the milk bowl and the slit in the vine! Almanzo's milk pumpkin grows bigger than any other pumpkin in the field!

Once the first frost hits, and the pumpkin vines turn brown, your giant pumpkin can be harvested and weighed! And then, of course, turned into soups, pies, muffins, and more!

Theme Gardens

Theme gardens turn regular old vegetable patches into places of wonder! Imagine planning a garden bed as a future pizza or a bowl of salsa! Grab the whole family for a brainstorming session and come up with a few of your favorite themes to plant! Some ideas are:

- Pizza Garden: Basil, oregano, garlic, and tomatoes
- Salsa Garden: Cilantro, tomatoes, jalapeños, and onions
- Salve Garden: Calendula, comfrey, yarrow, and lavender
- Ice Tea Garden: Peppermint, lemon balm, hibiscus flowers
- Bird Seed Garden: Sunflowers, amaranth, and millet
- Thai Garden: Eggplant, hot peppers, and Thai basil
- Snacking Garden: Snap peas, lemon cucumbers, green beans, and strawberries
- Pie Garden: Strawberries, blackberries, and rhubarb

Homestead Family Profile: Isis Loran
West Kootenays, British Columbia, Canada

Kids ages five months, two, five, and eight years

Photo by Isis Loran

Q: What are your homesteading goals, and how do your children fit into those goals?

A: When I started homesteading, I wanted to try gardening, but when we had our first baby I began to want to grow and make healthy baby food. As the kids got older that evolved into growing a lot of food for them, growing the varieties they love to eat, and making our garden area fun to play in as well. I really want our kids to understand where their food comes from. I've had many losses of seedlings along the way, but our kids are involved from sowing to growing, weeding, and harvesting. Now we learn wild foraging too; it's my goal for the kids to know how to acquire as much food as possible without the grocery store.

Q: What challenges come with homesteading with very young children?
A: Balance is really hard, especially as I work from home and homeschool. I think realizing you won't get everything accomplished that you want to is important. Being adaptable to what the day, week, or season brings, too. The kids are involved as much as they can be, but they can also make it harder to get many tasks done. It's the hardest with babies and toddlers. I've found the older ages are able to help out and do more around the garden and homestead.

Also, getting interrupted with questions all the time can be frustrating. Although it's great for them to be constantly learning, sometimes I wish I could just get something done. I've learned that mother self-care is super important. I ask hubby to watch the kids so I can have a whole thirty minutes to recharge myself. Even if I only get it every few days, it's better than nothing.

"A huge benefit of homesteading has been seeing the kids eat veggies that they wouldn't touch at the grocery store. They love choosing colorful and fun varieties that they get to grow and eat. They still, to this day, love eating radishes from the garden but won't eat grocery store ones." —Isis Loran, FamilyFoodGarden.com

Homestead Family Profile: DaNelle Wolford
Phoenix, Arizona

Kids ages twelve and fourteen

Photo Credit: Weed 'em & Reap, www.weedemandreap.com

Q: When did you start homesteading, and what made you begin?
A: In 2009 we were ready for a change, both in health and in financial dreams. We decided to purchase an acre of land in our hometown and began homesteading. My son had asthma and I had a host of issues. We were able to improve our health all while learning to grow our own food!

In the beginning it was all about what we could do minimally, and it's slowly grown over time to what it is today. We used to have a tiny garden, but it keeps growing each year. We believe growing our own food is healthier for us—and because our kids eat that food, they have a responsibility to help.

They are always happy to help and honestly we feel lucky to have such grateful kids.

Q: How do your kids help on your urban homestead and what kind of oversight do you provide?

A: Our kids take care of the goats, sheep, and chickens. They feed and water, milk the animals, and gather eggs. I mainly focus on the garden and enjoy mastering that. My husband oversees the kids' chores and together we make it all possible. [The kids] definitely have mastered skills that most people (today) won't master in their lifetime. For that, I'm proud. I'm hopeful my kids will take with them the ambition to do whatever they want, if they work hard enough.

Q: What is your biggest challenge when it comes to homesteading with children? How do you overcome this?

A: The kids often forget details, which can make all the difference in the end. We try to make sure our kids are trained on the routine and ensure they are doing the entire process. The time factor comes into play when there's a big project to complete—like building a fence or starting a garden. Maintenance is always easy and only takes us about thirty minutes per day. We love it!

"Give [kids] responsibility and expect them to be capable enough to get it done. You'll be surprised how great they'll be at doing it!" —DaNelle Wolford, WeedEmAndReap.com

CHAPTER SIX: CARING FOR ANIMALS

When asked what his favorite thing to do on the homestead is, my seven-year-old son, Everett, replied, "Play with animals." Animals have been an integral part of our homestead life since 2000, the second summer on our Oregon homestead. Our children were born into a rhythm that was crafted by the needs of our farm animals: Morning and evening chicken chores, morning milking, afternoon electric fence moving, and midday visits to all

of the creatures to say hello. Over the years, our homestead has swelled to include ducks, pigs, cows, sheep, goats, bees, and chickens and shrunk back down to only chickens, but the gifts that our animals provide are always plentiful.

In this chapter, I'll share some of our experience raising animals with the help of children. I'll offer suggestions on how to get started with animals at home and talk about how to care for animals in ways that are safe and fun.

Which Animals Are Right for Kids?

Animals are a great way for kids to learn responsibility, care for another living creature, and practice observation, patience, and problem solving. If you have the space and inclination, I'd be the first to tell you to go ahead and get a few creatures! But knowing which ones will be a good fit for your children's age range and personality is a bit more challenging. Different animals have different temperaments, and so do children. My daughter desperately wants a farm animal that she can cuddle with, but her favorite animals on our homestead are chickens. The chickens don't seem to "get" cuddling, so it's not a great match for her desires. (Meanwhile, our cat meows at anyone who walks

by, begging for a bit of scratching, but I digress.)

If you were interested in raising animals that are kid-friendly, my first suggestion would be chickens. They are interesting to observe, give valuable products, and are relatively easy and affordable to care for. Ducks would be a close second, but I find ducks to be messier, and sadly, more prone to predation. I would feel comfortable letting my seven- and ten-year-olds be 100 percent in charge of the routine care of chickens and ducks.

Although we have never raised them ourselves, I have heard from many homesteading families that rabbits are another great choice for kids. Their size and care requirements are kid-compatible, although I have heard that rabbits can vary in their desire to be touched or petted. Rabbits can be raised for fiber, manure, or meat, so make sure that your entire family is on the same page about the purpose for which the rabbits are being raised.

Small livestock breeds such as Nigerian dwarf goats are another

excellent choice for older children. These goats are about the size of a medium dog, yet they still produce creamy, delicious milk, and children's hands are ideally sized to milk from the small teats of Nigerian dwarf goats. Although goats require a bit more upfront investment in terms of fencing, feed, housing, and purchasing the animals themselves, breeding goats for freshening may produce a larger herd than you desire, in which case, the sales of offspring may balance out the cost.

We have raised pigs, lambs, full-size goats, and Jersey milk cows as well, and I felt less comfortable letting the kids manage these animals without adult supervision, due to their size and, in the case of the goats and cows, horns. Still, each of these animals was delightful to be around. There is simply nothing cuter than a baby cow or baby goat, and they are just the right size to snuggle with a small child. Ultimately, you should feel comfortable making choices that are right for your family, and just as one person might be a golden retriever person, and another a poodle person, your family may find itself drawn to the spirit of a particular farm animal.

If you're new to raising animals, but still want to share them with your children, you may want to seek out a local mentor. Mentor relationships work best when they are reciprocal; perhaps your family helps muck out the chicken coop in exchange for some guidance on how to build a coop of your own. Where we live, 4-H and FFA experiences give children broad exposure to, and training in how to raise, all varieties of farm animals. We've experienced some of our more memorable homestead moments when we've all learned about how to care for a new animal side by side.

Raising Chicks

One of the most rewarding homestead experiences for our children has been raising chicks. I mean, who can resist those tiny balls of fluff? Come springtime, you can find the most common breeds of young chicks for sale at farm and home stores. However, if you are looking for a more specific breed or heritage breed chicks, you may wish to order online from a reputable hatchery (the Additional Resources section of the book has a few suggestions). We have found Buff or Lavender Orpingtons, Wyandottes, and Easter Eggers to be very kid-friendly and docile.

Before you get chicks, be sure to have the necessary equipment on hand. At minimum, young chicks will need a draft-free, predator-proof environment (such as a large box in a garage), water in a shallow dish, chick mash (feed), and bedding. Young chicks also need to be kept warm. A mama hen would do this by tucking the young chicks under her wings. Human parents will need to use heat lamps to keep

temperatures of 95°F for their first week of age, 90°F for their second week, 85°F for their third week, and so on, reducing by five degrees until the chicks are five or six weeks old, or until you arrive at ambient temperature (this is one reason we like to wait until a bit later in the spring to bring young chicks home).

Children love tending to chicks, and this is a fabulous time to let children be responsible for the caring of an animal. Children can feed and water chicks, watch their behavior, or lay new bedding. We also encourage our kids to gently handle the chicks from the time they are young so they become familiar with the

chickens and the chickens with small humans. Be sure to teach children to wash hands after handling chicks.

If you already keep hens and a rooster, you may want to allow a broody hen to sit on a clutch of fertilized eggs and hatch chicks. When we notice a hen going broody (she will sit on eggs most of the day, and get rather aggressive if you try to remove the eggs from under her), we move her to a smaller coop where she can sit in peace for twenty-one days.

The benefit of allowing a broody hen to hatch her chicks is that your family can truly observe nature in action. Broody hens are excellent mamas, making sure

their chicks stay perfectly warm and dry, teaching them to forage for food, and protecting them from other birds. On the other hand, Mama Hen is less thrilled when little human hands snatch her chicks away for some cuddle time. We try to respect Mama Hen's protective authority, but also allow our kids to hold the chicks each day for socialization and human interaction.

Of course you can always purchase an incubator and hatch your own chicks at home! If you choose to do that, you'll need to obtain fertilized eggs, which you can ask around for locally, or via the magic of the Internet, purchase online.

Try eBay for small family operations that will send you an assortment of fertilized eggs.

Chickens are often cited as the "Gateway Animal" and it's so true! Our first flock of chickens led to meat birds a year or two later, followed by meat and dairy animals of all manners. At this point in our homesteading journey, it's the kids who "egg" us on to more chickens. Don't say I didn't warn you!

Safety in Caring for Animals

Something I think about a lot, especially when we have younger visitors to our homestead, is safety around our farm

animals. While smaller creatures may just inflict scratches or pecks, larger animals can cause serious injury to humans. We talk to our children quite a bit about how to be safe around homestead animals.

A good rule of thumb when handling any animal is to wash hands after coming into contact with them. We have a hand-washing station outside that feeds water from a rainwater catchment, but you could easily set up a similar station with a water dispenser that has a spigot. We use a small squirt bottle of liquid soap and keep a hand towel nearby for easy

washing without having to come indoors. This makes it much more likely that we all wash our hands as frequently as we should!

We also keep a close eye on animal enclosures such as fences, gates, and electric fences. Animals are very good at knowing when gates are left open or electric fences are shorted out. I can't even count on my two hands the number of times that we've had to wrangle pigs, goats, sheep, or cows that have managed to escape from what we thought was "bomb-proof" fencing! If this happens, the kids know that they should immediately return to the house and tell an adult!

Even with smaller animals, like chickens, there are always risks. Roosters can become aggressive toward humans, seemingly overnight. I was once chased several hundred feet by a rooster that was trying to attack me; he was in the stew pot the next day, because on our homestead, we have no room for this kind of behavior.

Larger animals require discernment based on careful observation. Our first Jersey cow was very prancey and unpredictable with her movements while she was pregnant. We decided to let the kids brush her from the other side of her food trough so there was no chance of an accident happening. When she gave birth to her first calf, her personality changed immediately into a loving, affectionate pet. We felt much more comfortable letting the kids enter her pen to brush her, or spend time in the pasture with her. Her second calf, a bull, was calm and sweet until he approached sexual maturity, at which time we no longer felt safe with the kids in proximity.

In general, animals like routine, quiet voices, and slow movement. Small

children are not always the best at these things! We love the experiences our children have been able to have caring for animals, but we always keep safety at the forefront of our thoughts, and keep a close eye on our animals for any changes in behavior.

Butchering Animals

Some of my most controversial moments as a blogger have arisen from sharing photos of my children participating in the butchering process. Eating meat, killing animals, allowing kids to watch—these are very personal decisions, and my goal is not to convince you to eat meat or butcher animals alongside your children. However, I will share some of the reasons we have chosen to bring our children into the process of butchering, even when it might feel uncomfortable.

As a meat-eater, I feel it is my responsibility to understand where meat comes from and how it gets from pasture to plate. We enjoy raising our own meat, and have ample space on our homestead to do so. Whether we're raising our own pork, beef, chicken, or lamb, we honor each animal by giving him or her the best life possible on our homestead, a quick death to ensure as little pain as possible, and full use and appreciation for their meat, bones, skin, and organs.

In completing this circle of life right here on our homestead, our children

have the opportunity to learn valuable lessons and skills. Among them: Animal husbandry, responsibility in the form of chores, animal behavior, anatomy, food storage and preservation. We all experience love and loss.

Because we are a small homestead and not a large farm, we have time to form intimate connections with the creatures that share our life. We name them, we observe their sweet, unique personalities, and we fall in love with the animals we intend to eat. So, how do I reconcile killing the very creatures with whom I've forged a deep connection?

Why do I encourage my children to participate in their care, knowing that we will all have to say good-bye?

Because I choose to eat meat, I am 100 percent committed to raising meat in the most healthy way possible—outdoors, with ample sunlight, on pasture for as much of the year as possible, and with as few chemicals as I can muster. And because I have poured sweat, tears, and love into the process of raising meat, I value every single bite. The meat we raise becomes a precious gift that sustains our family.

If you choose to raise meat and butcher it at home, with your children, here is what has made the process go smoothly for our family. Because we use a rifle for a quick kill, we have not yet allowed the kids to be present for the slaughter. This is something we will re-evaluate as they have gotten older and we have trained them in necessary safety procedures. We do not force the kids to participate in butchering, but encourage them to bring their curiosity to the table. The most amazing conversations have happened while skinning a rabbit, removing the organs from a lamb, or cutting and wrapping pork. This is biology in action, and kids are often incredibly eager to watch or help.

Depending on the ages of your children, they may be able to actively participate in the butchering process. My role on butchering day is often wrapping and labeling cuts of meat; this is a job that a ten-year-old child could certainly take on. Properly trained and supervised, a teen would make an excellent assistant or head butcher. Even young kids can be in charge of "scrap buckets" and collect bits of meat for sausage making into plastic bags.

We do our best to keep the memory of the animal whose life we took alive. Some families may have a different approach, but we will often name the creature as we eat it, saying, "Osage's meat is so tender and delicious." This feels like gratitude and appreciation to me, and keeps our family connected to our food source.

Homestead Family Profile: Justin and Rebekah Rhodes
Asheville, North Carolina

Kids ages three, six, eight, and ten

Photo Credit: Christy Zbylut

Q: How has homesteading evolved for you, from the time that you started, to now?
A: It started as a cheapo way to get groceries, but has turned into a passion for good health, having a connection to our food, and even as a way to care for the earth and teach our children how to work. We started out growing "conventional" organic. We used tillers and sprays. Now, we let animals and nature do all the work by applying principles of permaculture.

Q: How do your four kids help with animal care on the homestead?
A: All the kids work and play beside us as they desire. It's their choice, but if they work, they get paid. For example Jonah, our nine-year-old at the time, let

out the turkeys in the morning and put them up at night. He didn't always want to do it, but he knew he would receive a turkey to sell at the end if he lasted. A hundred dollars will buy a lot of LEGOs for a nine-year-old.

Q: What is your biggest challenge when it comes to homesteading with children? How do you overcome this?

A: The hardest part is actually letting the little ones help. We can do it so much faster and better. I just have to remind myself that I'm growing something much, much, more important than food. I'm growing children, and our deepest hearts' desire is to see our children one day provide for themselves, their families, and contribute to society in a positive way. And that only happens by learning how to work.

Q: How have your children grown and benefited from homesteading?

A: Well, for one, they end up eating dirt and connecting with the earth, which benefits their immune systems. Also, it's a natural way to learn about the "birds and the bees" since animals mate in the broad daylight. We actually keep an eye on the bull to make sure the cow stands and they connect. Mating becomes something to celebrate because we're going to get a calf or chicks or whatever. The potentially awkward topics of birth and death come naturally as well, since they see that on a regular basis on the farm.

"Let them help, don't worry about planting in straight rows, buy 25 percent more seeds, and don't sweat it if they over-sow, lose some seeds, or trample some produce. Remind yourself of the bigger picture . . . of your bigger goals for that child's life." —Justin and Rebekah Rhodes, AbundantPermaculture.com

Homestead Family Profile: Ashley Browning
Southwestern Montana

Kids ages ten and eight

Q: How are your girls involved in homestead chores?

A: When we moved onto our homestead, my daughters were two and four years old; at that point the girls definitely came around with us to do the chores—feeding the chickens, milking the cows, collecting the eggs, or cleaning out the coop—but they did not have chores of their own.

My oldest is a pretty responsible kid, so it was easy for her to take on more chores as she got older. When she was six, she took over the care of the chicken flock: feeding them, watering them, closing up the coop, collecting the eggs. She decided she wanted to have a chicken business selling eggs. She bought fifty-five hens—we got her started with feed until she started making money, but now that's her full responsibility.

You definitely have to take into account the personality of the kid; with my youngest we struggled to have her take on responsibility. Now she has a worm business, raising red wiggler worms. She saved up her birthday money and bought some red wigglers from a gentleman in town. She's been feeding them and taking care of them, in addition to feeding the dog and taking care of the cats.

Q: What is your biggest challenge when it comes to farming with children?

A: The easiest *and* hardest part of homesteading is when death happens on the farm. It happens a lot, and we don't sugarcoat things, but we do feel so deeply for our animals, even when we know that we're going to eat them. My daughter has a lot of chickens that are really old and not laying, but she doesn't want to talk about killing them. On the other hand, we butchered three pigs on the farm this year, and the kids did not even bat an eye.

Q: What advice would you give to someone who would like to share homesteading with his or her kids?

A: Involve your children as much as you can. If they are little, put them in a carrier on your back—I milked cows with my youngest on my back. Show them every single thing you can. Don't be afraid. That goes for all aspects of homesteading, even the stuff in the kitchen—fermenting, baking, cooking, going out in the woods and foraging. Having my kids along makes me learn so much more!

"Involve your children as much as you can. Show them every single thing you can. And also ask your kids, 'What do you think we should do in this situation?' This allows them to think critically, and they'll remember these lessons for the rest of their lives." —Ashley Browning, Red-Fox-Farm.com

CHAPTER SEVEN: PREPAREDNESS

Watching the recent wildfires in California, my mind turned to preparedness. If your family got a call to evacuate in minutes, would you be ready? I know mine wouldn't! This real-life wakeup call led me to think about how to prepare my family for all manners of the unexpected, from weather-related emergencies such as floods or tornadoes, to wilderness survival situations, to life's everyday challenges. As homesteaders, we already have a very broad skill set to help us weather the unexpected, but we can always be better prepared. This chapter will offer some practical advice and hands-on learning on how to prepare kids for unforeseen situations, without making preparedness seem scary.

I think of preparedness as starting with a self-sufficient mindset and then developing a skill set that will help you overcome challenges. A preparedness mindset is not necessarily the same as always keeping an eye out for impending disaster, but it is thinking practically about how you'd respond when things go wrong. For instance, I recently called my mom and dad, both of whom live on the east coast, to make sure they were prepared for a coming snowstorm followed by an extreme cold snap. Fortunately, they had at the ready pre-prepared foods, flashlights, a propane fireplace, warm blankets, and a plan to stay at home. In our home, our woodstove, water filter, and freezer and pantry full of food mean that we can keep ourselves warm, hydrated, and fed no matter the weather outside, and our root cellar gives us a safe place to go in case of tornado warnings.

A preparedness mindset often includes a bit of redundancy—for instance, keeping bottles of water at the ready, and also having a portable water filter, or including both a poncho and a large plastic bag in an emergency kit in case of rain. A preparedness mindset also involves planning and communication. Coming up with family evacuation or safety plans is a great idea, but unless everyone in the family knows how they work, they will not be effective. Finally, a preparedness mindset includes testing and refining your plans so they go smoothly if you need them. Involving kids in the entire process of emergency preparedness is empowering for them—they will know exactly how to take care of themselves and help the family if needed.

Create a 72-Hour Kit

In a real-life emergency, you may only have minutes to prepare for an evacuation. Even if you were blessed with more time to safely move to a different location, wouldn't it be nice to not have to worry about the basics? A 72-hour kit is designed to help you navigate three days of uncertainty by containing essentials such as food, clothing, water, and your most important belongings. Once kids

are old enough to help pack a backpack, they can gather and pack the essentials in their 72-hour kit. As a family, the 72-hour kit should be one part of a broader emergency plan that should be practiced on a regular basis. (YouTube has some great videos of families preparing to evacuate in ten minutes. I sat down with my kids and we watched them together so they understood what an evacuation might look like.)

A 72-hour kit can be contained in a backpack, suitcase, plastic storage tote, or other container, as long as you can easily carry and transport it. Inside your kit, you will want to have:

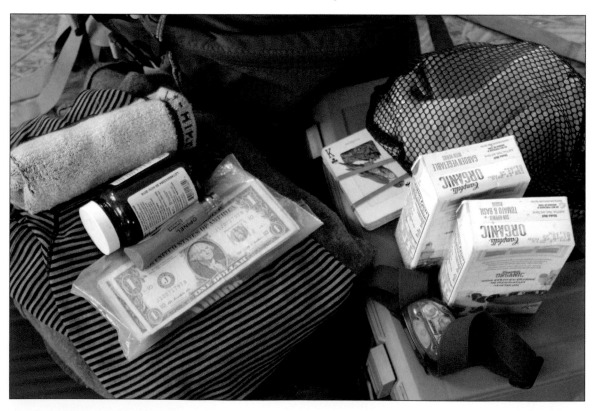

- Water: FEMA recommends storing at least one gallon of water per person per day, which means that you'll need at least three gallons per person for your 72-hour kit. You should also have a plan on how to treat and purify water in case you run out.
- Food: If you need to leave your home, you'll need easy-to-prepare nutrient-dense food. While I have never tried them, I have heard that meal replacements and dehydrated foods have come a long way! Cooked, canned food that can be eaten cold, if necessary, is also a smart addition to your 72-hour kit.
- Utensils, dishes, bowls, and a stove to heat food or boil water.
- Important documents: Plastic file folders are perfect for storing portable copies of your most important documents such as birth and marriage certificates, insurance information, wills, and important phone numbers.
- Fire starting supplies: This is one area where redundancy is important. At least two methods of fire starting should be part of your emergency kit—for instance, matches and lighters.
- Basic tools: At minimum, a knife, ax/hatchet, and shovel.
- A tent and sleeping bags: If you need to evacuate by car, it can be used as

your shelter, but warm blankets are still good to have on hand.
- Medications: Any prescription or over-the-counter medication taken regularly.
- First aid kit: A robust first aid kit for home and for your car. This should include bandages, burn cream, antibiotic ointment, etc.
- Flashlight with extra batteries.
- Weather alert/emergency alert radio (hand crank is best!).
- Stuffed animals or small toys for kids' comfort.
- Optional: A few lightweight, portable games or decks of cards to keep everyone calm and entertained.

There are dozens of websites online that share recommendations and checklists for 72-hour kits. You may want to find one that is specific to your region (for instance, if you're in a desert climate, you probably want to pack more water than indicated here, and perhaps items like sunscreen or a sunhat).

Once your kit is prepared, place it in an easy-to-get-to location that everyone in the family knows about and be sure to update it regularly so food, water, and medications do not expire.

Basic Knots

Knots are not only supremely useful, but they are also great for kids' developing minds and hand-eye coordination. Kids

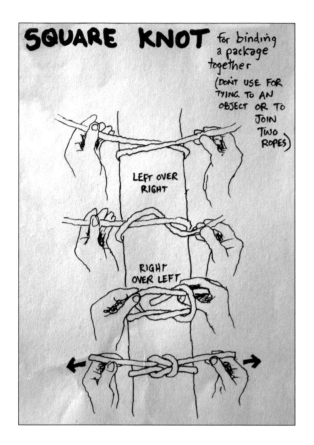

SQUARE KNOT for binding a package together (DON'T USE FOR TYING TO AN OBJECT OR TO JOIN TWO ROPES)

LEFT OVER RIGHT

RIGHT OVER LEFT

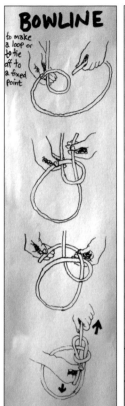

BOWLINE to make a loop or to tie off to a fixed point

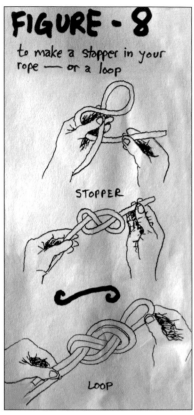

FIGURE - 8 to make a stopper in your rope — or a loop

STOPPER

LOOP

tend to jump right into learning knots, as they are much like puzzles to be solved! Here are a few basic knots—Square, Bowline, Figure Eight, Clove Hitch, and Sheet Bend—that can be used for camping, boating, fort building, or just for fun!

Knife Skills and Whittling

A great way to practice knife skills that could be valuable in a survival or preparedness situation is by whittling, or carving with a knife as the main tool. This, of course, is the type of skill that is

very age- and maturity-dependent. My son had just turned six when we gave him his first knife, but we know him to be very calm, careful, and focused. A good guideline is that kids should be able to understand safety rules and sit calmly before given their first knife.

Knives should be large enough to provide good grip, but small enough to be stored easily. We bought our kids locking blade pocketknives made by Opinel. At three and three quarter inches when closed, these knives fold and fit safely in a pocket when not in use, and

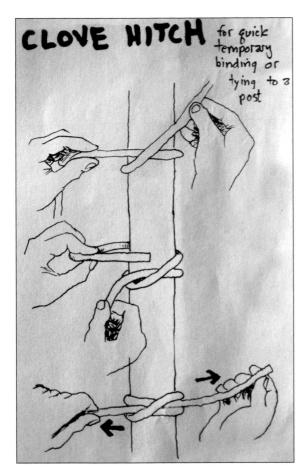

CLOVE HITCH
for quick temporary binding or tying to a post

SHEET BEND
for tying two different ropes together

are a good size for small hands. We've been very pleased with the quality of these knives. They look, feel, and act like a larger knife (meaning they are very sharp!), so it's important to teach proper knife skills and safety.

It may sound counterintuitive, but it's actually safer to start with a sharp blade than a dull one. Sharp blades allow the knife to glide through the wood, rather than having to apply excessive amounts of force that may lead to injury. Help your kids find some soft wood with no

knots to begin carving practice. Either head out into the backyard and pick up a few sticks, or try one of these woods: Pine, birch, willow, walnut, pecan, alder, maple, cherry, or apple.

Knife Safety

My kids went to a nature day camp this summer where they had the opportunity to practice their knife skills. The safety rules were clear and concise, allowing a large number of children to work with sharp knives without anyone getting injured! In our house, the safety rules are equally clear and if they are not obeyed, the knife gets taken away: 1) The knife is never open when you are in motion. 2) Do not begin to use the knife until your "circle of safety" is clear of other people. If you extend your arm and rotate it in an imaginary circle around your body, that is your circle of safety. 3) The knife will slip at some point—that is a given. To protect your fingers and body, the knife should never be pointed in a path that would result in it cutting your leg, fingers, or body. 4) For beginners, the knife should always be pointed away from the body.

Once kids have learned the safety rules, it's time to practice. We started with some small branches that still had their bark attached. The kids removed the bark by carefully and smoothly running the blade along the branch, turning it after each stroke. Once the bark is removed, your young whittler can move to the tip of the branch and practice making a sharp point. This kind of carving is quite intuitive and the point is to get comfortable moving the knife over the wood.

Carving Apple Faces

We practiced our carving skills this autumn by making apple faces. Although we were working with butter knives instead of sharp carving knives, the act of carving faces made our kids more comfortable using knives as a tool; that skill can easily translate to carving with wood.

The process of carving apple faces is quite easy: Peel a large, firm apple, and then let your imagination run wild as you use a butter knife to carefully take away pieces of apple flesh. We then attached a bit of string to the apple stem and hung it near the woodstove to dry. After a few weeks, the face really begins to take shape; after a few months, we were left with hard-as-rocks, withered and weathered faces!

Working with Fire

Kids seem to be naturally attracted to fire, like the moth to flame. Because fires are useful tools for heat, light, cooking, and boiling water, we've tried to give our kids the empowering experience of working with fire, while making sure they understand fire safety. We had the unique experience of living without electricity for a year and a half while we built our house, with beeswax candles as our primary light source, and our neighbors exclusively use candles for light, so from a very young age, our kids have been around adults modeling the responsible use of fire as a tool.

At home, we have a campfire ring as well as a woodstove, so we have many opportunities to teach the kids how to safely light fires. We started to allow the kids to help at the woodstove when they were three or four years

old, beginning with how to clean the glass with an ashy newspaper and how to crumple up newspaper for tinder. As they got a bit older and had better hand-eye coordination, they were able to lay the kindling in the cold firebox, and eventually light the match and start the fire with adult supervision.

Outdoors, we have clear safety rules about lighting campfires: It needs to be a day without wind, the ground needs to be bare, and there needs to be a pot of water nearby to put the fire out completely. There will always be an adult nearby to lend assistance, if needed. We put less emphasis on the "correct" method of lighting a campfire (although you could certainly rouse a good argument debating the merits of the "Teepee" versus the "Log Cabin" with campfire pros), and more emphasis on what you need to easily light a fire: dry kindling, a pile of tinder, and a fire-starting implement. While there may be some who disagree with our parenting choices, we actually encourage the kids to build small fires for learning and play. They have boiled natural dyes and "potions," fired clay pots, and made charcoal on their campfires, and have acquired useful skills for either a fun camping trip or a survival situation.

Homestead Family Profile: Tessa Zundel
Southwest Missouri

Kids ages fifteen, thirteen, eleven, nine, and four

Q: How did your preparedness journey begin, and how are your kids involved?

A: Preparedness is actually part of my religious culture. As a kid I remember attending meetings where some of the topics included self-sufficiency, education, caring for the community, and even growing a garden. So, for me, it's just always been my normal. To *not* live a preparedness lifestyle seems unusual to me.

Photo Credit: Tessa Zundel

Once I started having kids, we were busier, of course, but there were also more hands and more opinions and more eyes for each project. We have so many intelligent voices in our family and they've all been raised to work. So, whereas I have *more* food to store, *more* gardens to grow, *more* materials to gather, I also have more help, more ideas, and more points of view.

Kids help you remember the great *why* of a preparedness lifestyle. Without my children constantly pointing out the wonder of our every day, I'd burn out fast, because preparing is a lot of work. They make me take breaks for funky dancing in the kitchen. They remember to sing songs around the outdoor fire while we labor over our dinner. And they always, always find pretty chicken feathers when we muck out the coop.

Q: In what ways do your kids share the work of the homestead?

A: We have a rotational chart for daily chores, so no one has the same thing every day. For the land and animals, here's what we're doing right now: My son is in charge of livestock feeding, watering, haying, and administering herbal wormer. My teen daughter is usually in charge of baking, various food preservation projects, and meal preparation. She has a natural way with animals and is usually called into action when we have a sick or laboring animal. My eleven-year-old is in charge of the sourdough culture and baking. Both she and her teen sister do a lot with dairy fermentation too—yogurt, cultured cream, paneer, etc. My nine-year-old is in charge of the egg collection and she also keeps an eye on the chickens and all the animals. My four-year-old is in charge of feeding our outdoor cats and dogs. She's also charged with playing with them.

Once the growing season is on, we'll all have work outside too. We're in a new house so we have to build gardens from scratch. None of us likes pulling weeds, but we all seem to work pretty well together otherwise in the garden.

All of the kids have daily domestic chores too. Things like dishes and laundry and sweeping. We all think that stuff is super boring so we rotate the work so no one has to do the same thing every day. We know we can't just *not* do it, but, as Erma Bombeck pointed out, no one ever had a religious experience scraping burned cheese from a toaster oven. We do all that work because having a clean living space keeps us happy and healthy so we can do the fun work of homesteading and home education.

Q: What is your biggest challenge when it comes to homesteading with children? How do you overcome this?
A: Time! Between education, church and community responsibilities, classes, and home life we're stretched thin every day. If we let it, that can be frustrating. The way I see it, though, life is hard and we can either laugh or cry about it. We've decided to laugh since crying gives us a stuffy nose.

The best way we know to keep our priorities straight while still being flexible enough to enjoy the journey is to keep to our chore schedules, school schedules, homestead schedules. If we always have a plan, then we can always refocus when we get sidetracked. We've learned to roll with the punches of the seasons and the things that up and go wrong or fall apart. However, having a plan and clear goals for each day means we recover quicker when we get knocked down. Sure, most days I'm so busy I fall asleep in my clothes. But I'm never, ever bored.

Q: Is there one specific example that you can share about how your children have grown and benefited from hands-on homesteading and preparedness training?

A: My eleven-year-old was recently butchering a turkey with me since that's where she landed on the chore chart for that day. It's not a chore she would normally volunteer for—indeed, most poultry harvesting days find her inside tending the younger kids rather than being out with us in the blood and the guts. That day, though, we were only processing the one turkey and she needed the experience.

We talked about the mechanics of where to slice and how to carve off the bone. We chatted about what to do with the skin, the meat and the bones. We prepared dog food from the skin, cutlets for our family dinners from the meat, and healing broth from the bones. We talked about why it's important to know where your food comes from and how to provide for ourselves. We laughed about how grossed out she was at the feel of the skin. We felt a great deal of pride the next night when we had a homemade stir-fry with our fresh turkey meat.

I think the biggest result I see in my children living this lifestyle is that they're grateful. They don't take as much for granted as they might. They're used to work as a way of life and are easy to please with good food, baby animals, and campfires. Simple pleasures aren't lost on them. And that makes my parenting job a lot easier.

"Don't wait for enough money or enough time or enough familial support. Go slowly, be smart, and don't try to go anywhere without your family on board. But don't get stuck in the planning and perfecting phase and never actually make a change. And give yourself a huge learning curve. I figure after about fifty years of practice I might be actually ready to live a preparedness lifestyle in earnest. In the meantime, I do the best I can and enjoy the days I have." —Tessa Zundel, HomesteadLady.com

Homestead Family Profile: Lisa Bedford
Texas

Kids ages sixteen and eighteen

Q: When did you start your preparedness journey, and what made you begin?
A: In early 2009, when the recession began. I keep up with current events and when I began reading about bank failures, businesses shutting down in huge numbers, and massive numbers of home foreclosures, I knew our family and our business could be next. I try to be proactive as a general rule, so it made sense to begin researching what I could do, as a mom, to mitigate the effects. That led me to survival and preparedness websites and soon we were stocking up on food and taking other measures to be better prepared.

In the beginning, I didn't have much of a plan. I just knew I wanted to get extra food stored as fast as possible, teach the kids how to handle various emergencies on their own, have an emergency kit in the car—I did a *lot* of prepping in a very short amount of time! As pieces began to fall into place, I slowed down a bit with buying things and stocking up and began spending more time developing skills and knowledge.

Q: How are kids involved with your preparedness lifestyle?

A: As older teenagers, they are pretty independent. They both know how to cook from scratch, shoot a gun, what it means to be situationally aware, etc. In the beginning, we just included them in everything we were doing, from grinding wheat for our flour to going to the gun range, and kept everything very matter of fact. There was never much fear or panic on their part—these were just fun, new family projects and outings. Whatever we did, we kept in mind the age, abilities, and maturity of our kids and provided the appropriate supervision and training.

Q: What advice would you give to someone who would like to share preparedness with his or her kids?

A: Decide what steps you want to take in order to become better prepared, in general. This could be building a food storage pantry, storing water, taking steps to better secure your home, saving money, etc., and then include your kids whenever and however you can. Don't worry about explaining to them *why* you are doing these things if they are very young or very impressionable. Just have fun stocking up on extra food, adding backyard chickens or bees, or putting together emergency kits/bug out bags. Take them camping and hiking to teach some basic survival skills. Go on bike rides around town so they begin to learn how to navigate, locate safe places, such as tornado shelters and homes of family/friends. Think about what you want them to know and then find ways to teach it so that it becomes an adventure and family bonding time. It won't take long before they will have an impressive skill set and, more importantly, a mindset that includes independence and confidence.

"Think about what you want them to know and then find ways to teach it so that it becomes an adventure and family bonding time. It won't take long before they will have an impressive skill set and, more importantly, a mindset that includes independence and confidence." —Lisa Bedford, TheSurvivalMom.com

CHAPTER EIGHT: HERBAL WELLNESS

While harvesting some culinary sage from our garden this morning, I plucked off a large leaf and handed it to my son, Everett, to smell and taste. "Mom," he said after a moment of consideration, "I want to make a potion with herbs." Thus began a wandering tour of the herbs in our garden, stopping to taste and smell edible plants (peppermint and lemon balm were his favorite), and ultimately collecting a handful of healing herbs for a "cure everything" salve that Everett decided to make.

I share this snapshot of our day because it exemplifies the best way I've found to share herbal medicine and homemade remedies with my young kids: safely, organically, and playfully. Plants have powerful medicine to share with our children, and I try to make learning about herbs and medicinal plants fun and informative at the same time.

Unlike my journey into homesteading, which has felt like a dive off a cliff into a cold, deep pool, I've moved into herbalism with a bit more of a stick-your-toes in-the-water approach, learning two or three new herbs each year. Still, even knowing how to prepare and use a small handful of herbs has been incredibly empowering for my whole family. My kids know to reach for the echinacea tincture or cold care tea when they feel a bug coming on, and they use herbal healing salves to soothe their itches and skin irritations. They can identify plantain and other common backyard herbs in the field, and even enjoy eating stinging nettle!

In this chapter, I'll talk about some ways to use the plants and herbs in your garden and backyard to introduce your kids to the wonders of herbs and to stock your medicine chest with homemade healing remedies. I'm a mom who is passionate about taking my family's wellness into my own hands, but I'm not a professional herbalist, so rather than telling you how to cure, diagnose, or treat, I'll point you toward the practical, sharing suggestions on how to incorporate herbs into your family's wellness efforts and offering projects and kid-approved recipes to prepare with your young ones.

A note about safety: It is important that kids be supervised when using herbs, especially if they are very young. Children should be taught to always check in with you before handling or ingesting any plants. I will be suggesting the use of herbs that are generally considered to be safe for children, but please consult your family physician if your child takes medication or has a health condition that may make the use of herbs contraindicated.

The Medicine in Your Backyard, Garden, and Kitchen

Herbal medicine can be found all around us—in the backyard, in our gardens, and in the kitchen. Sharing herbs with your children begins with getting to know some important plant allies, and planting, foraging, or sourcing fresh or dried herbs. Whenever safe and appropriate, encourage kids to touch, smell, experiment with, and get to know herbs. For instance, my kids love making "smelly packets," which are basically pieces of cut-up fresh herbs folded into toilet paper that they carry around and sniff! In creating smelly packets, my kids have learned which herbs are safe to touch, which are aromatic, how to harvest leaves, and that herbs offer incredible sensory experiences in addition to their healing properties.

Getting to know medicinal plants in the field—what they look like, where they grow, and when they should be harvested—can be done in any environment, wherever you live. I'll share a few of my favorite healing plants that you can find in your backyard, garden, or kitchen.

In the Backyard

Wander through your backyard for a few minutes. Chances are, you've already passed (or stepped on) backyard herbs that have medicinal qualities. Some of the most common backyard weeds— dandelions and plantain, for instance— can be used for healing. Others, as we learned in chapter 3, can be eaten as food. Wild plants with healing properties can be found in meadows, forests, stream beds, parks, and roadsides, but of course it's important to observe the same wild harvesting guidelines and safety rules that you would follow when foraging.

Later in this chapter, we'll use dandelion flowers and plantain leaves to make a soothing salve. Both are easy to identify and locate, so be sure to invite your kids to do the harvesting with or for you!

Dandelion (*Taraxacum officinale*)— We've already added dandelion greens to our foraged salad for a slightly bitter springy flavor, but dandelion flowers can also be used in making salves, oils, and lotions. Because dandelion flowers are thought to have pain-relieving properties, use them in remedies and products that soothe aches and heal rough skin.

Plantain (*Plantago major*) is a common backyard plant whose leaves are said to contain anti-inflammatory and antibiotic properties. It is frequently used to stop the itch and pain of insect bites and stings and its soothing qualities make it perfect for use in our healing salve.

In the Garden

Healing herbs grown in the garden serve multiple purposes: They bring beauty to the garden, especially herbs that have showy flowers like echinacea (coneflower) or rose; their flowers attract pollinators (I love planting oregano, basil, and anise hyssop for this purpose); and

their roots, leaves, and/or flowers can be harvested to make herbal remedies.

An herb garden can be as small as one or two plants in a container, or as large as your imagination allows! I've successfully started many herbs from seed, and a good garden center will offer many more options. I love growing a variety of kid-friendly herbs, including calendula, lemon balm, and anise hyssop, all of which are great additions to herbal tea blends or salves.

Calendula (*Calendula officinalis*) is a beautiful all-purpose flower that brightens up any garden. My kids

love to pick the petals and put them in salads (they are edible!) or create small bouquets. Calendula's gentle healing qualities make it useful for minor cuts and scrapes and other skin irritations.

Lemon balm (*Melissa officinalis*) is a member of the mint family that is known for its self-sowing abilities and intense lemony flavor—my kids love it in sun tea as a lemonade alternative. Lemon balm is considered a calming herb that is thought to reduce stress and anxiety, improve sleep, and soothe indigestion.

Anise hyssop (*Agastache foeniculum*) is a beautiful edible and medicinal plant whose licorice flavor makes it a yummy addition to herbal tea blends and sweets. It is also known to have anti-inflammatory and antimicrobial properties, which makes it a great choice for reducing itching and treating minor wounds.

In the Kitchen
Perhaps the simplest way to share medicinal herbs with your children is to invite them into the kitchen. Some of the most commonly used kitchen herbs (and vegetables) have healing qualities that make them great additions to your herbal first aid kit. A few examples are garlic, onion, thyme, turmeric, ginger, sage, and

cayenne. As you cook together, start to mention some of those healing qualities. Later, use kitchen herbs like garlic or ginger to create remedies such as the "fire" cider recipe in this chapter with your kids.

Ginger (*Zingiber officinale*) is well known as a winning ingredient in cakes and cookies, and even as a tummy-soother, but its anti-inflammatory, antifungal, and antioxidant properties make it a powerful food-medicine. Ginger is such a kid-friendly flavor that can be added to herbal teas and sodas, fermented foods, and more.

Garlic (*Allium sativum*)—Okay, I'm going to be honest here: My kids hate when I sneak garlic into food and can spot a minced piece of garlic in their dinner from a mile away! The strong flavor that so many of us adults go crazy over can be a bit intense for little ones, but garlic's antioxidant, antifungal, antiviral, and antibacterial power makes it worth exploring with your young herbalists!

Harvesting and Drying Herbs for Medicine

When you harvest fresh herbs for home use, the rules of harvesting are very much like the rules of foraging: Harvest ethically, be 100 percent sure which plant you are harvesting from, understand which part of the plant is the most potent, and know when to harvest. Depending on which herb you are using, different parts of the plant—leaves, flowers, roots— should be harvested.

Flowers, such as chamomile and calendula, should be harvested just before full flower, and can be snipped off the plant with small scissors, or the blossoms pinched off with your fingers. My kids love heading out to the garden with a small harvesting basket and pinching off blooms! If you're harvesting leafy plants like basil, lemon balm, or peppermint, it is best to harvest before the plant blooms, and easiest to use scissors or pruners to cut stems, and then strip the leaves off with your fingers. Roots such as dandelion or echinacea should be harvested after their foliage fades and carefully dug up with a spade, and the roots washed well. Harvesting roots can be really fun for kids because it feels a bit like a treasure hunt!

If you cannot grow, forage, or find the herbs that you're looking for, there are many wonderful distributors of dried and fresh herbs. I'll share a few of my favorites in the Additional Resources section at the end of the book.

If you will not be using your fresh herbs right away, you can preserve them for future use by drying or dehydrating. Herbs can be hung upside down in small bundles or laid flat on a screen to dry out of direct sunlight. Using these methods, the herbs should be

completely dry within a week—you'll know they are ready when the herbs crumble easily in your fingers and you feel no moisture.

If you live in a more humid climate, you might want to use a food dehydrator with the thermostat set between 95°F and 115°F, checking for dryness in one to four hours.

Stocking Your Herbal Medicine Cabinet

If you're new to sharing herbal medicine with your family, my suggestion is to start with three types of remedies: immune boosters, skin soothers, and everyday health enhancers. Immune boosters are the remedies you're going to reach for when you or your kids feel a bit under the weather, or to keep a cold at bay. In this chapter I'll share how to make a fire cider and a delicious elderberry-echinacea syrup. Skin soothers are going to help you through the everyday itches, minor cuts, scrapes, bruises, and irritations. You'll learn how your family can infuse herbs in oil, and then how to create a healing salve that is gentle enough for everyday use. And lastly, three fun projects in this chapter—infused honey, an herbal tea party, and hand-sewn dream pillows—will bring the soothing, healing qualities of herbs into everyday life.

Homemade Soothing Salves

A salve is a healing balm that is typically made with a few simple ingredients: oil infused with healing herbs of your choice, beeswax, and perhaps some essential oils or vitamin E oil. Many healing plants, including some that are thought of as weeds, such as plantain or dandelion, can be infused to create a salve.

Grow a Salve Garden

Making salve begins with growing, harvesting, or sourcing herbs. I like to involve my kids from the beginning by growing a salve garden. A salve garden can be as simple as two or three plants, or as complex as you'd like. The wonderful thing about healing plants is that so many of them make gorgeous additions to flower beds.

The following plants are easy to grow—many of them will reseed in the garden or grow vigorously as perennials—so they are great choices for a salve garden: calendula, comfrey, echinacea, yarrow, peppermint, lemon balm, and lavender.

What Kind of Salve Should You Make?

Of course if you add wild-harvested and purchased herbs to the mix, you can come up with an infinite number of salve formulas to address common complaints. A few of my favorite combinations of herbal healing salves are:

- Gardener's Hand Salve: calendula flowers, plantain leaves, comfrey leaves (Note: Comfrey should be used externally only, and some medical professionals caution against using it on broken skin)
- Itch-be-Gone Salve: jewelweed leaves and stems, plantain leaves, rose petals
- Sore Muscle Rub: echinacea leaves, flowers, or root, dandelion flowers (Optional: add ginger or cayenne to make this blend tingle a bit!)
- All-Purpose Healing Salve: calendula flowers, yarrow leaves, plantain leaves, lavender flowers

Making homemade salve is a great project to do with kids, or with friends. Salve making can get a bit messy, so it's advisable to have all materials and ingredients on hand so you can work quickly. Start by preparing an herb-infused oil in advance with the following recipe.

Create an Herb-Infused Oil

Herb-infused oils can be used on their own (think a soothing massage oil) or used to make other herbal preparations. Although there are faster methods of making herb-infused oils, when working with kids, I use the solar infusion method because it is a safe and fun way to infuse the oil with the herb's properties. To make an herb-infused oil, start with herbs that have either been completely dried, or have been allowed to dry at least overnight, as too much moisture can cause the oils to go rancid

1. Place your dried herbs in a clean, dry quart-size mason jar.
2. Fill the jar with a carrier oil—olive, coconut, or jojoba oils are good choices—to at least one inch above the level of the herbs.
3. Stir or swish the jar, then tightly cap and set the jar in a warm and sunny area. Shake the jars at least once every few days.
4. After three to four weeks, strain the oil through cheesecloth, squeezing to remove all of the oil. Alternatively, you can strain only the amount you need at that time, and leave the remaining oil to continue infusing.
5. Store oil in a glass jar in a cool, dark place, and use within one year. A few drops of vitamin E oil can be added to prolong shelf life.

Make Your Salve

I like to use the following recipe to make salve, knowing you can scale up or down as you wish. The process of making salve does involve warming oils over the stove. I regularly make salve with my ten-year-old daughter—she and I actually have a salve-making business—and she is able to participate safely in all steps of the process, including warming the oils. Younger children may help by getting containers ready, creating labels, or adding drops of vitamin E oil. Use your own best judgment.

Ingredients:
1 cup of infused oil
1 ounce of beeswax (grated, chopped, or shaved OR use beeswax pastilles)
3–5 drops of vitamin E oil
10–15 drops of essential oils

Equipment:
A double boiler, either purchased or improvised with a bowl in a pot of water
Cheesecloth
Tins or jars for your finished salves
A scale to weigh your ingredients

1. Create a double boiler by placing a stainless steel bowl inside a larger pot of water. Place over medium heat and begin to bring water up to a simmer.

2. Measure your infused oil into the stainless steel bowl and add the beeswax. To make a softer salve, add a bit less beeswax than recommended; to make a harder salve, add a bit more beeswax.

3. Heat gently in the double boiler until the beeswax melts completely. While the beeswax is melting, get your tins or jars ready.
4. When melted, turn off the heat and add the vitamin E oil and essential oils. Stir gently to combine.
5. Carefully pour into your containers and allow to cool completely. I like to cool them at room temperature because I have found that if the salve cools too quickly, it may crack. Label your creations and store out of direct sunlight.

It's a great idea to make a few different sizes of salve that you can tuck into various places—the bathroom cabinet, the car, and your purse—for easy access.

Cold Care Syrup

Some of my earliest memories involve swallowing foul-tasting spoonfuls of penicillin to treat frequent bouts of strep throat. As an adult I stayed away from all forms of syrupy medicine until the kids and I started making this homemade cold care syrup. The cinnamon, cloves, and ginger in this cold care syrup make a delicious addition to the herbal immune-boosting power of elderberries and echinacea. We like to prepare for cold season by making a large batch of cold care syrup to store in the refrigerator. For immune boosting, most sources recommend that adults take up to one tablespoon of the syrup per day, while children should take one teaspoon. For acute illnesses such as colds or flu, take the syrup several times per day. Note: Honey should not be given to children under one year.

Ingredients:

- 1 cup whole elderberries (You can also use ⅔ cup elderberry powder or 2 cups fresh elderberries)
- 2 tablespoons echinacea root
- 2 tablespoon fresh ginger root
- 1 cinnamon stick
- ½ teaspoon whole cloves
- 3½ cups water
- ¾–1½ cups raw honey (sweetened to your personal preference)

1. Place all ingredients *except* honey into a heavy saucepan and simmer over low-medium heat for 30–45 minutes.
2. Strain the liquid using a mesh strainer or cheesecloth.
3. Allow the mixture to cool until it is just warm to the touch. Add honey and stir until well mixed. Refrigerate until use.

Rose Petal Honey

Last summer our family spent a few weeks in June and July near the ocean, just as the beautiful beach roses (*Rosa rugosa*) were in bloom. Rose petals have qualities that can, among other things, help uplift emotions and bring calm. Add their sweet, intoxicating fragrance, and the fact that their petals and hips are edible, and you have a perfect plant to share with kids. We wandered the sand dunes, collecting bags of bright pink petals that we brought home and laid on paper towels to allow any insect stragglers to crawl out and for the petals to dry. We reserved a handful of the fragrant petals to make a rose-infused oil for salves, and added the remaining petals to honey.

Infused honey is a perfect topping for baked goods like scones or biscuits, as a drizzle over ice cream, or stirred into tea. You can also use the recipe below to infuse other herbs and spices, such as lavender, sage, rosemary, cinnamon, or ginger.

A few safety notes: Honey should not be given to children under one year. Because roses, beautiful as they are, also have thorns, younger kids should be shown how to avoid thorns while harvesting petals. Use the foraging guidelines from chapter 3 to make sure that the petals you harvest are from a safe source, and be aware that the roses you buy from a supermarket or florist are often treated with chemicals that would make them unfit for consumption.

1. Place a handful of dried rose petals in a pint-size mason jar.
2. Cover the petals completely with a mild flavored honey, such as a wildflower blend or a clover honey, and stir gently to allow air bubbles to escape.
3. Allow the roses to steep in the honey for days or months! The flavor will only intensify the longer the petals remain.
4. Rose petals are edible, so feel free to leave the petals in the honey. However, if you would like to strain out the petals, first gently warm the jar of honey by placing it in a bowl of warm water. Strain the honey through a mesh strainer and be sure to lick the strainer clean!

Herbal Tea Party

You know that sweet, warm, relaxed feeling that a hot cup of tea can provide? Kids relish that feeling too. Hot herbal tea with a touch of honey and milk is one of my kids' favorite beverages, especially at bedtime. It is easy, fun, and inexpensive to make your own tea blends at home. Whether you harvest and dry your own backyard herbs or purchase tea ingredients in bulk, a fun activity for kids is a make-your-own-tea party. This would be the perfect activity for my ten-year-old daughter and her friends!

First, gather a selection of kid-friendly herbs and flowers. Some of our favorites include:

- Peppermint
- Lemon balm
- Chamomile
- Calendula flowers
- Rose petals
- Nettle
- Lemon verbena
- Borage flowers
- Lavender
- Fennel
- Licorice
- Orange peels
- Cinnamon stick
- Raspberry or blackberry leaf

Place each herb in a bowl and allow kids to scoop small spoonfuls of herbs into a mason jar. Invite them to decorate a label and create a name for their custom blend. Wrap up the party with cups of warm tea—maybe sweetened with some rose-infused honey!

Kid-Friendly "Fire" Cider

A "fire" cider might sound a bit scary, but never fear, it's simply an herbal remedy that has a base of apple cider vinegar, and usually contains onions, garlic, cayenne, horseradish, and honey. Devotees of this spiced-up cider vinegar take a "shot" daily to boost the immune system. Spicy ciders are incredibly warming, not to mention antiviral, antibacterial, and anti-inflammatory, so consider adding them to your family's winter routine.

You might be thinking that this sounds a bit intense for kids! Fortunately, there are ways to keep the health benefits of a fire cider intact, while making the flavor a bit more appealing to kids. You might:

- Combine equal parts strained spicy cider and olive oil for a zesty salad dressing
- Dilute the finished spicy cider with apple juice
- Add orange peels, cinnamon, and lemon zest or juice to your concoction
- Add some "fire" cider to a cup of herbal tea
- Drizzle it over steamed vegetables in lieu of soy sauce

As always, choose the freshest ingredients possible when making your "fire" cider. Making your own spicy cider is not an exact science, so feel free to alter this recipe to fit your tastes!

Ingredients:
½ cup fresh peeled and shredded ginger root
½ cup peeled and diced turmeric OR shredded horseradish (Note: If you decide to use horseradish, make sure an adult does the shredding, and consider wearing sunglasses or eyeglasses!)
1 onion, chopped
10–12 cloves of garlic, minced or crushed
2 fresh jalapeño peppers, chopped, or 1 teaspoon cayenne pepper powder
Raw apple cider vinegar
Raw honey
Optional additions:
Lemon zest and juice
Cinnamon stick
1 teaspoon dried echinacea root
Orange peels
Elderberries
Dried rosemary or sage

1. Place all of the ingredients except the apple cider vinegar and honey in a quart-size mason jar.
2. Pour in enough raw apple cider vinegar to cover the ingredients completely, cover with a mason jar lid (preferably a plastic one because vinegar can cause the metal lids to rust), and shake well.
3. Place your "fire" cider in a cool location for three to four weeks so the ingredients can steep.
4. When ready, strain the cider through cheesecloth and either discard the herbs or add them to a soup or stir-fry.
5. Stir in raw honey, tasting until you've reached a desired level of sweetness. You may want to make a smaller batch for kids with a bit more honey! Store in a cool location.

Health and wellness should be fun, but it also pays to create a routine around herbal wellness. Invite your kids to make a morning routine of taking a spoonful of cider to kick-start the day!

Sweet Dreams Pillow

A sweet herbal project that can be shared with kids as young as four or five years old is sewing sweet dreams pillows. These are small pillows—the size of tooth fairy or eye pillows—that are filled with a variety of rest-inducing herbs to promote easy sleep and sweet dreams. I have a very small lavender-filled one that I use as a post-yoga eye pillow that my kids love to borrow!

Older kids can use a sewing machine and fabric of their choice. If you have any old bedsheets lying around, they would be perfect for repurposing! Younger kids can practice their sewing skills by making a sweet dreams pillow out of wool felt. For an extra special pillow, use the instructions in chapter 9 to dye white wool felt with your favorite plant dye!

Some of the very same herbs that make such lovely herbal tea blends can be used in a sweet dreams pillow. I love to use buckwheat or rice and lavender as the filling, along with a combination of soothing herbs such as chamomile, catnip, lemon balm, rose petals, and hops.

Equipment:
Buckwheat or rice for filling
Herbs of choice
Fabric
Needle and thread
Sewing machine
Scissors

1. Prepare your fabric for sewing. If you're using cotton, wash, dry, and iron it before sewing. Wool felt that has been dyed should be thoroughly rinsed.

2. Cut the fabric into two identical shapes. Squares and rectangles are easiest, but you could also make whimsical shapes such as hearts or moons. Wool felt is particularly easy to shape.

3. Pin the "wrong" sides of the fabric together and stitch along the edges, making sure to leave a two-inch opening to fill the pillow.

4. Flip the pillow right side out and fill it with your buckwheat/rice and herb mix. If your young sewer is hand-stitching a pillow, you may want to create an inner sack for the filling so it doesn't spill out between the stitches.

5. Carefully sew up the open area. Your pillow is now ready to place in the bed, or under your pillow.

Homestead Family Profile: Rachel Jepson Wolf
Southwestern Wisconsin

Kids ages eleven and fifteen

Q: How has homesteading evolved for you, from the time that you started, to now?
A: When we started homesteading I wanted to do it all. Right now! Within the first year of buying our homestead we brought on goats, sheep, cows, bees, rabbits, chickens, ducks, and quail. We planted a big garden, then an orchard, and set to work cutting our own hay and foraging in the

Photo Credit: Rachel Jepson Wolf

woods and grassland for medicine and food. (Whew!) But as the first few years unfolded I realized that we truly couldn't do it all. No one can. There are only so many hours in the day, and there are always trade-offs. Inevitably something will slide when you take on so much. We needed to prioritize and choose what fit our family best.

Many long conversations, walks in the pasture with our various flocks, and family meetings later we made the decision of which pieces to let go of and what we wanted to keep. It was hard, but necessary. We slowed down. We exhaled. We found a better fit. Doing just a couple of things well feels better than doing a mediocre job of many, and we now have time for family play, housekeeping, homeschooling, and business work.

Q: How are your children involved with herbalism and herbal wellness?
A: Both of my kids are passionate about foraging and using wild plants as food and medicine, so we often go out together to gather and explore. As they learn things on their own they in turn teach me about plants or uses for plants

that I was unaware of. It's a beautiful balance of learning and discovery—together.

Together we grow, harvest, and dry herbs, and make remedies. Recently while visiting my family, someone was cut taking a fall on some rocks. My daughter immediately looked at me and whispered, "Yarrow. She needs yarrow!" And off she set to forage an herb to help comfort her cousin. When she was unable to find yarrow, she returned with a handful of chickweed, another appropriate choice for the injury at hand.

I realized then how second nature these skills have become for them. This knowledge is no longer something that I shared with them: it is authentically their own. And I'm so grateful that they have grown up in an environment where they can absorb so much.

Q: What kinds of homesteading tasks do your kids participate in?
A: Since we brought home our first chicken the kids have been involved in daily homesteading chores. When we had sheep the kids helped with daily watering and winter hay. These days they do all of the daily small animal chores (bedding, food, water, collecting eggs, etc.); and also help with cutting and baling hay when needed in the summer.

I believe that there is a job that is a match for every member of the family. I help my kids figure out how they can do their share, while operating within their skill set and comfort zone. I empower my kids to be honest about what they are capable of and push their own limits, while respecting who they are and how they're wired. Take chicken butchering, for example. There's no denying that it's a hard day, but one in which each of us has found our place. My child who doesn't have a stomach for the butchering first catches the birds, then heads to the house to cook meals for the rest of the family. He also takes care of dishes and cleanup, making butchering day so much easier for the rest of us.

Q: What is the *why* behind your commitment to homesteading with your kids?
A: I'm a firm believer in the importance of learning real, hands-on life skills. To grow up knowing how to forage nettle, grow green beans, milk a goat, make cough syrup, butcher a chicken, bake bread, and extract honey sounds like a

pretty solid start in life to me. We've moved so far from these skills as a culture, and I felt it was time we returned. Because of growing up on a homestead, I'm often surprised by what my children have absorbed without being directly taught.

I also think that growing up on a homestead, raising your own food, and foraging your own medicine gives you a deeper appreciation for these things. We don't take them for granted. We are less likely to waste our food when we know the name of the animal on our plate, or planted the seeds ourselves that grew the vegetables.

Q: What advice would you give to someone who would like to share homesteading with his or her kids?

A: If you are still in the dreaming stage of your homestead, learn and grow together wherever you are. Even in an apartment in the city you can make space to learn and grow side by side with your child. Use this time to figure out what your family dreams and goals are for your homestead—what your children's dreams are. If your child is really into goats or flowers or green beans, delve deep into that learning together so that when your homesteading dreams come true everyone is on board and eager to get to work. Once you find your farm, empower them to follow their own dreams, and participate their own way. Life will be more satisfying and more joyful when you do.

"This empowering of my kids comes down to how I am wired as a mother. I bristle at the notion that I must force my kids to participate in something that they are uncomfortable with or resistant to. So we find a way to make it work for everyone. This means they have grown up knowing that everyone does their part, but what that looks like can vary so that everyone feels good about their contribution." —Rachel Jepson Wolf, https://rachelwolfclean.com

CHAPTER NINE: HANDMADE HOMESTEAD CRAFTS

If you've ever gone on a walk with young kids and come home with a pocket full of treasures, then you know the appeal that the found objects of the natural world have to kids. Sometimes these treasures end up on the shelves and desks of our home, and sometimes they are used to create nature-based crafts that celebrate the beauty of the natural world and the turning of the seasons. The following projects minimize purchases in favor of natural supplies that you can find in your backyard, on a walk, or in your garden.

Corn Husk Doll

I treasure the brief period of time when sweet corn is available at our local farmers' market. The kids get to work shucking the corn as we adults boil a pot of water. A few minutes and some butter and salt later, our hands and faces are greasy and our bellies full of a quintessential summer treat. With the pile of corn husks left behind, we can make sweet little corn husk dolls to celebrate the harvest season.

Equipment:

Corn husks (If you do not have corn husks at hand, you can purchase husks that are sold as tamale wrappers)
Embroidery thread or thin twine
Scissors

1. Gather a small pile of husks of equal length to form the body of the doll. We used four husks in these project photos. If you are using dried husks, it helps to pre-soak them in water for a few minutes to make them more pliable.

2. Tie some thread about an inch from the top of the narrow end. Grabbing hold of the wide edge, fold two of the husks over the narrow tied end. This will become the head. Wrap a section of embroidery thread around the "neck" area and tie a square knot. This is a great opportunity for kids to practice their basic knot skills!

3. Set the doll aside for a moment and gather one or two husks that will form the arms of your doll. Roll the husks into a tube and tie a few threads around the wrists. Tuck the tube (arms) under two layers of the doll's torso and wedge it under the neck. Secure the waist of the doll just below the arms with a second piece of embroidery thread.

4. If you'd like your doll to wear pants, you can snip up the center of the husk "skirt" and secure the two sides into legs at the ankle. Otherwise,

trim or shape your doll's skirt as you'd like.

5. For a special added touch, wrap another piece of husk crisscross around her torso for a beautiful shawl!

Ella decided to also craft a bonnet from another husk, and in a later version, she even made baby corn husk dolls and attached them to a mama doll with a corn husk sling!

DIY Black Walnut Ink

Since moving to the Midwest, we have developed a bit of a love affair with a common tree, the black walnut (*Juglans nigra*). Black walnuts are allelopathic, which means that the tree releases chemicals from its roots that can harm other species, which can be challenging if you are trying to grow a garden or fruit trees nearby. However, in my mind, the benefits of black walnuts far outweigh this disadvantage, and if you are lucky enough to live near a mature black walnut tree, you can reap the abundant gifts of the black walnut: nutmeat, syrup, and husks for natural dyeing and homemade ink making.

Making your own ink out of black walnut husks is a perfect project to do with preschool and kindergarten age children, although older kids will enjoy it as well. Creating black walnut ink weaves nature exploration, tree identification, measuring and pouring, fine motor skills, and writing and drawing effortlessly into a fun activity.

An easy time to identify black walnut trees is in the early summer, when the young nuts are large and bright green in color. Take note of these trees so you can come back in the autumn to harvest the nuts and in the winter so you can tap the tree to make syrup (learn how in chapter 3)! Black walnuts fall to the ground when they are ripe and ready to harvest, and because they are so large and easy to

spot on the ground, they are very easy for kids to collect.

A warning: Black walnuts make a fabulous natural dye, and as such, can stain your hands and clothing. Take care to wear old clothing and/or gloves when working with mature black walnuts and to place newspaper beneath your paper when writing.

Equipment:
Black walnut husks
Large nonreactive pot
1 cup white vinegar
Wire mesh strainer
Cheesecloth
Storage container for finished ink
Optional: vodka for preserving ink

1. Collect black walnuts from the ground in autumn. We will be using the outer husk, not the nut, which means that you can keep the nuts to cure and eat! If you have harvested partially rotted black walnuts whose husks have already begun to soften, then they are

ready to use. If not, place the walnuts in a large pot of water overnight to allow the husk to soften.

2. In a large nonreactive pot, preferably one dedicated to dyeing, cover crushed black walnut husks with water and add one cup of white vinegar.

3. Bring the pot to a boil, then simmer for one to two hours. We like to do this over a campfire outside, but you can boil it on the stovetop, again, being very aware that black walnut will stain.

4. After simmering, allow the black walnut slurry to cool, and then strain two times to remove all solids; first through a wire mesh strainer, then through a piece of cheesecloth.

5. Store your black walnut ink in a container with a tight lid and label. If desired, you can preserve your black walnut ink with a bit of alcohol (cheap vodka will work fine). Gather some rooster feathers to fashion your own quill and dip into your homemade

ink! You can also use watercolor paintbrushes and use the ink as paint.

If you do not have black walnut trees in your region, you may want to experiment with making berry ink. The following berries will generate nicely colored ink in the pink to purple range:

• Pokeberries (Note: Although pokeberry makes a gorgeous hot pink ink and dye, the berries are toxic, so exercise extreme caution using these berries with children.)
• Raspberries (both red and black)
• Blackberries
• Black cherries

To make berry ink, place two cups of berries (fresh or thawed frozen) and ½ cup white vinegar in a nonreactive pot and simmer for ten to fifteen minutes. Allow to cool, and strain as above.

Natural Dyeing

Ella and I went to our first natural dyeing class when she was six years old. We came home with a beautiful array of silk scarves and pieces of wool that had been dyed with some of the plants we commonly find on our land: Tickseed coreopsis, goldenrod, pokeberry, comfrey, Osage orange, and black walnut. Since then, we've tried to do a community dye event each autumn, usually in someone's outdoor kitchen. Children are always invited to participate, but to be honest, the full process of natural dyeing involves multiple steps, many large pots of boiling water, and a lot of waiting, which can cause young kids' attention span to wane.

I'll share a bit about the natural dyeing process here, and then offer some suggestions on how to make this process more kid-friendly, so your entire family can share this experience together. For those who want to dive into learning more about dyeing with plants, I'll include a few of my favorite books in the Additional Resources section.

Natural Dyeing Basics

The leaves, roots, and bark of many types of plants can be used to dye plant (cotton, linen, etc.) and animal (wool, silk, etc.) fibers. To improve the lightfastness, washability, and range of colors, dyers will often treat fibers before dyeing with a mordant, which is a substance that helps fix the dye color to the fiber. Both chemical and natural mordants can be used; some examples are aluminum sulfate, copper sulfate, rhubarb leaves, and oak galls.

After dyeing, fibers can also be treated with a modifier that will change the final shade to something completely different than when the fiber left the dye pot. Often this is done by adding a product that alters pH. Again, there are chemical modifiers and naturally derived modifiers such as citric acid, copper sulfate, ammonia, white vinegar, or wood ash water. The use of mordants, plant dyes, and modifiers enables home dyers to achieve a wide range of colors from the exact same dye plant. For example, the use of turmeric root as a dye yields a bright yellow color, but the addition of modifiers and mordants enable you to also dye in shades of brown and brownish-green.

To simplify the dyeing process, while still getting to experience the joy of producing color from plants, I like to choose dye plants that don't require a mordant. I also dye without using further modifiers. The trade-off is a more limited palette of color, and also dyed fibers that may be slightly less colorfast, but the process is notably streamlined and more hands-on for kids. Here are a few common and easy to find dye plants that don't require a mordant, along with the color they will produce:

- Elm bark: Pink-tan
- Coffee grounds: Chocolate brown
- Blackberry leaves, canes, and shoots: Light yellow-brown
- Blackberry fruit: Light pink
- Rhubarb roots: Bright yellow
- Turmeric roots: Bright yellow
- Onion skins: Bright yellow
- Walnut husks: Light to medium brown

Equipment:
Plant matter for dyeing
An assortment of nonreactive pots or
    glass jars
Mild dishwashing soap
Wool or silk
Wire mesh strainer or cheesecloth

1. Prewash your yarn or silk scarves in warm water with a teaspoon of mild dishwashing soap per gallon of water to remove any traces of dirt or oil that may inhibit the uptake of the plant dye. Before washing yarn, wind it into a skein and handle gently to avoid matting or felting. Rinse thoroughly several times.

2. Although dyers will typically simmer their plant matter for hours to extract the plant dye, I'm going to recommend using either of the following two methods that are safer and more inclusive for children. I'll walk through the process of dyeing wool yarn, but you could also use the same method to dye silk scarves.

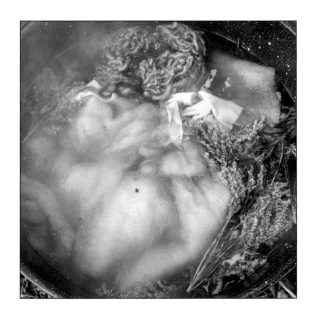

One Pot Cool Dyeing—To use this method, add your plant materials to a large pot, and add boiling water until the plant material is completely covered and the water level reaches to no more than half the pot. Allow the plant material to steep for an hour or so before filling the pot with cool water and adding your prewashed and wet fibers. At this point, you can let your fiber sit in the dye bath for as long as needed until you've achieved the desired color.

Solar Dyeing—This is a great way to use the energy of the sun to create beautiful hues in a process similar to making sun tea! Fill a gallon capacity glass jar with your dye plant material and enough water to completely cover the plant matter. Set in a sunny location in your yard for a few days until a nice bright color develops.

Strain the plant matter out of the liquid using a wire mesh strainer or cheesecloth, and then place your prewashed and wet fibers into the dye bath. Set the jar back in your sunny spot and allow the fibers to take up the dye for a few days. Alternatively, you could place plant dyes and fiber in the glass jar together and make this a one-step process. The disadvantage would be that you run the risk of getting small pieces of plant material embedded in your yarn, so perhaps save this process for easy-to-rinse silk scarves!

3. Allow your fibers to cool, and then rinse your yarn or silk with a bit of

mild dish soap until the water runs clear. Keep in mind that if you're working with wool, you do not want to change water temperatures abruptly, as it can cause shrinking or felting.

4. Hang your dyed yarn or silk scarves on a clothesline to dry thoroughly, and then store the skeins out of direct sunlight. Have fun using the silk scarves for imaginative play, or learn to knit using a skein of hand-dyed yarn.

Beeswax Candles

When we built our house, there was about a year's time between when we actually began living in the house and when our solar electricity was fully installed. During that time, we used beeswax candles to light our home. Beeswax candles are beautiful to look at with their bright yellow glow, and because they are made of nontoxic material, they are safe to burn around little ones. They are also easy to make at home for your own use, or for gifts. Because beeswax is flammable, younger children should be closely supervised when melting beeswax, but older kids could easily tackle this project on their own. Because candles require a large quantity of beeswax, it is worth seeking out local beekeepers who may be able to sell you beeswax for much less money than you'd spend in a craft store or online.

Equipment:
Beeswax
Wick (#4 braided cotton wick will work well for up to four-inch diameter candles)
A container in which to melt the beeswax

4 ounce canning jars or other small containers

Wooden skewer or chopstick

1. Melt your beeswax in a double boiler or designated slow cooker. I made an improvised double boiler out of a diced tomato can in a bowl of water. It's important to note that beeswax is challenging to remove from tools and surfaces, so it's a good idea to comb the thrift stores for beeswax-designated supplies.

2. While the wax is melting, set your canning jars (or other containers) on a piece of parchment paper and prepare the wick by cutting it into five-inch pieces and wrapping the top around a wooden skewer or chopstick.

3. At this point, I like to pre-dip my wick into a bit of melted wax to help keep the wick straight. Next, carefully pour a bit of melted wax into the bottom of your canning jar, and then lower the wick until it touches the center of the bottom of the jar. Allow the wick to cool in place for about five minutes.

4. Slowly pour the remaining beeswax until your candle is at the desired height. Allow to cool slowly, preferably overnight. Trim the wick to a quarter-inch high before lighting. The first time you use your candle, it's preferable that you burn it for at least one or two hours.

Beeswax Dipped Leaves

When my kids were younger, they would run back to the house, eager to show me the perfect fall leaf they had found. That one perfect leaf turned into dozens, and pretty soon I had a collection of beautiful brightly colored leaves. Preserving leaves in beeswax is a great way to capture the vivid reds, oranges, and yellows of the season in a garland of color. The first step, of course, is to find handfuls of perfect leaves! This is a perfect opportunity to get some warm clothes on, grab a few harvesting baskets, and take a walk in your neighborhood. Seek out leaves that are vibrant in color, but have already fallen from the tree.

Equipment:

Beeswax

A small slow cooker or a double boiler

Newspaper for your workspace

Clothespins or paperclips and some twine on which to dry the leaves

1. Using a double boiler or a small slow cooker, slowly melt beeswax. You can find beeswax online through Etsy or candle making suppliers, but a less expensive option is to seek out local apiaries that may be willing to sell you larger quantities. Because beeswax is flammable, always melt beeswax over low heat and supervise young children. Slow cookers, especially the mini versions that often come for free with the purchase of a larger pot, are easy to find in thrift stores and are excellent to have on hand for homestead crafting. Let any leftover beeswax harden in the slow cooker and reuse it next time!

2. Cover your working surface with newspaper. Guide kids in holding each leaf by its stem and then gently dip the leaf into the melted beeswax, and then lift it straight out.

Photo Credit: Kathie N. Lapcevic

3. Use small clothespins or paperclips to hang leaves to dry. My friend Kathie, author of the website *Homespun Seasonal Living*, uses cardboard boxes strung with twine to create an easy, mess-free spot to dry leaves.

4. Suspend individual leaves with a piece of thread, or create a garland by threading together multiple leaves. Hang them over a window to let light stream through your beautiful leaves!

Ice Lanterns

When we moved from Oregon to Missouri, the kids got their first experience of a true four-season climate. Instead of bemoaning cold winter weather, we have tried to embrace the ice and snow that winter offers. Sometimes that involves sledding or cross-country skiing, sometimes it is midday ice skating breaks, and sometimes it's creating ice sculptures and lanterns!

Ice sculptures came about somewhat accidentally as Brian and the kids were playing around our tiny hand-dug duck pond. Stomping around the pond, they cracked the sheets of ice that covered the surface of the shallow pond, and decided to turn them upright and create icy structures by sinking them into the snow in a very Andy Goldsworthy–sort of way.

We've also had great fun creating ice lanterns and sun catchers, made from the various containers of water around our homestead. To make an ice lantern, simply fill a (non-glass) container with water and set outdoors to freeze. When the water has frozen to about one half-inch thick, pour the remaining water out and tip the container over to carefully remove the intact cylinder of ice. Set

a lit candle under the ice lantern and enjoy the glow! We love making lanterns in five-gallon buckets of water, but you can use containers of all shapes and sizes; Try making ice lanterns by filling balloons with water and setting them out to freeze! To add an element of winter cheer, add greens and berries to the water before freezing.

Homestead Family Profile; Angi Schneider
Texas Gulf Coast

Kids ages twenty-four, twenty-two, twenty, seventeen, fifteen, and eight

Photo Credit: SchneiderPeeps

Q: When and why did you start homesteading?
A: We've grown some of our food and lived a simple lifestyle for most of our twenty-six years of married life. I have a hard time with labeling our life; we pretty much just try to be producers rather than just consumers. I like to feed my family good food and it can be very expensive at the grocery store, so we started gardening. In addition to gardening we keep chickens for eggs and bees for honey and wax. As we're getting older and our children are leaving home our food needs are not as great as they once were. We also don't have the helpers we once did.

Our goal with our children has never been to raise the next generation of homesteaders but to raise capable children who are a benefit to their communities. We believe that this lifestyle is the most natural way of teaching those skills. We also want our children to know where their food comes from. Each year we assess what our family's food needs are and what help we have and then decide what to plant. We've learned that we can't do it all, all the time, so we have to prioritize.

Q: How are your children living a handmade homesteading life?

A: We encourage all of our children to be creative and several of them have made money from woodworking and sewing. These are skills that they will always have and will benefit them in their adult lives.

When our third son was about thirteen he decided he wanted to keep bees. We had a friend who kept bees and agreed to be his mentor. When he was about fifteen he started doing bee removals with my husband's assistance. For the next five years he worked his bee business. He's now focusing on his college work and his bees are just a hobby again.

Over the years he's learned entrepreneurial skills such as pricing work, managing money, and marketing. He truly was the one in charge of the bees and his dad was the assistant. He's learned how to look grown men in the eye and not be intimidated when they tried to negotiate his price. At the same time, he's learned to look beyond the person and see the circumstances and decide when not to charge for his services.

He's gained a solid reputation in our community and the surrounding communities. Because of this he has several letters of recommendation for college from mayors and other civic leaders who have worked with him. Lastly, he's earned a lot of money. He's been able to purchase a vehicle and save money for college so he can pursue an engineering degree. He's a worker and has had several "real" jobs along with his beekeeping.

I don't think homesteading is the reason he's done as well as he has. He's a pretty driven person. But it did give him the opportunity to try new things, even crazy things like keeping bees at thirteen.

Q: What advice would you give to someone who would like to share homesteading with his or her kids?

A: Start small and invite them to join you. If your children are older, recognize that they may not enjoy the work as much as you do and that's okay. However, the whole family benefits from the homesteading lifestyle and everyone should have responsibilities in that lifestyle. We try really hard to assign responsibilities based on enjoyment, but that's not always possible; sometimes we just need more hands so everyone pitches in.

"The homesteading life gives so many great opportunities to teach the lessons and skills we believe are important as adults. Some of those skills are a good work ethic, being creative, and looking for ways to fix things instead of replace things." —Angi Schneider, SchneiderPeeps.com

CHAPTER TEN: WORKING AND LEARNING ON THE FAMILY HOMESTEAD

Perhaps our biggest joy and greatest challenge as a family of modern homesteaders is walking that delicate balance between working, learning, and playing on the homestead. In truth, they are usually one and the same, as much of our fun revolves around being in nature together as a family. Still, bills need to be paid, and kids need to learn reading, writing, and arithmetic, so we do our best to create seasonally variable structure to our days that allows us to devote time to each of these pursuits.

Working and learning on the homestead is the fabric of our daily life. There is a give-and-take between when our energy needs to be focused on the children, when we need to focus on our own businesses, and when the needs of the homestead take first priority over all. With two work-at-home parents and two homeschooled children, we have little division between work time, learning time, home time, or homestead time. Although we loosely follow a school calendar for formal homeschooling, our days more closely follow an agrarian calendar with periods of intense homestead focus in the spring for animal births and garden planning and planting, and late summer for fall gardening, harvesting, and preserving. We overlap this with an online business calendar whose busy season is the holiday shopping season of November through December, and rely on a period of rest in the winter months to recharge for the coming year.

Homestead-Based Businesses

My first home-based businesses were babysitting my next-door neighbors and three younger brothers as a preteen, followed by a short stint delivering papers in my suburban neighborhood. As a kid, it was natural to look for ways to take on responsibility and earn a bit of income—who else was going to fund my eighties addiction to neon and hairspray? Now I watch with a mixture of pride and amusement as my own children make plans for their own cottage industries. Starting with the classic lemonade stand at the age of five, Ella has since moved on to babysitting and co-creating an herbal salve business. Everett decided that he too wanted his own business venture, so he and I are making beeswax candles to add to our family Etsy shop, Acorn Hill Handcrafts.

Because my husband and I are both self-employed, it's not unusual for dinner conversation to steer to the topics of sales and marketing, with the kids chiming in with their ideas about new products or packaging. As often as possible, we have tried to involve them in the day-to-day of our homestead businesses. I love to get their input for writing projects, and Brian is always happy to have help polishing metal or adding tags to finished items. I love the connection that I feel to my children when we're working on a project together and they seem to enjoy the opportunity to contribute to the family in meaningful ways.

I view our homestead businesses as an extension of the type of learning that will help the kids grow into self-sufficient, creative adults. They know how to light fires, ferment food, grow a garden, and care for animals, and they also know how to think creatively about work and income. Of course, not every family has the desire to create homestead-based businesses, but if it is something that appeals to you, here's what has worked for us.

As early as they are able, we have invited the kids to participate in our homestead businesses as much as their interest and skill level allowed. For instance, when Everett was three years old, Brian was making and selling black walnut cutting boards made with wood from our land. Sanding the boards was something that Everett could help with that actually made a difference in our ability to ship our product. Ella, who was six at the time, was able to coat the boards with a nontoxic oil finish, and I helped wrap them and package the boards. We each had our own unique and age-appropriate responsibilities.

We also talk quite openly about finances in front of our children because we believe it is important to start learning about the responsible use of money early on. Before we began working in earnest

on Ella's Sweet Rose Salves business, we first talked about what we'd do with any income she received. After we covered all of her business expenses, together we decided to put one third of her earnings in savings, keep one third for her to fund special purchases (for instance, quality art supplies), and donate one third to a local arts organization whose building burned down last year.

Similar to our view on chores, there are certain family responsibilities that just have to be done and everyone has to pitch in. There are busy times when Brian really needs all hands in support of his blacksmithing business. In those times, we each find a way to pitch in and help. Additional business ventures, like the salves or the beeswax candles, are optional at this point, but once the kids decide to pursue a business, it is their responsibility to follow through and we will lend support as needed.

Many homesteading kids base their businesses on the animals they care for. Egg sales are a great example. Even if you have a small flock, there is usually a period of time in the spring when the hens are laying faster than you can eat up all the eggs! Gifting them to friends and family is a wonderful way to share the egg love, or kids can sell the excess eggs. Keeping small animals such as goats, rabbits, or bees is another possibility.

Homeschooling on the Homestead

Our children's educational path up until this point has been homeschooling, with a nature-based, Waldorf education focus. However, the lessons of the homestead are not only for the homeschooled! The simple fact that we homestead with our children has been more of an education than any curriculum could ever cover. In fact, most of our homeschooling "curriculum" revolves around the seasonal work of the homestead and the daily investigation of nature that is part of our everyday life. Cow birth during school hours, and walking through the woods after a fresh snow and identifying animal tracks? It's a real-life biology class! Gardening in the early morning, foraging for spring greens, and harvesting meadow plants for natural dye? Botany lesson! Even the tracking of essential homestead information like how much feed is left, or how many eggs the chickens are producing is math in action.

The best lessons I could ever hope to teach my children are to live a life full of curiosity and wonder, and to never stop learning; we model this every day as we marvel at the beauty around us, and seek out ways to broaden our knowledge of all things homesteading. We don't claim to be experts at anything except working hard and being willing to try new things. We try to expand our knowledge whenever possible by reading—there

are at least four homesteading books in my bedside queue—learning from local mentors, watching YouTube videos (oh, what did we do before YouTube?), and of course that good friend of ours, trial and error.

Homesteading teaches many valuable lessons that are not always learned in school. Patience comes from months of waiting for a harvest or years of waiting for a cow to give milk. Resilience comes from the hard knocks of daily homesteading life—birth, death, failure, miscalculation, pests, or weather. Wonder and awe come from the chirping of a newborn chick, the first blades of spring-green grass, and a rainbow over the lush green pasture. Responsibility comes from daily chores, tending garden beds, raising animals, mucking the chicken coop, and running a homestead business. Flexibility comes from knowing that weather will always trump the best-laid plans, and that a goat will give birth when she is good and ready! Kids learn each of these lessons just by being immersed in the homesteading lifestyle.

If I were to offer one suggestion for learning on the homestead, it would be to simply let your kids explore and create. Turn off the television, take away the tablet, send them outdoors, and let nature be their teacher. Cut back on commitments to allow them the space and time to follow their interests and offer whatever support you can. Maybe this support comes in the form of your time and assistance, or perhaps the support comes from another trusted adult mentor. Trust that kids are always learning, even if the learning looks a lot like building fairy houses for years on end.

When our kids were very young, we bought them kid-size versions of the tools that we most often used around them: shovels, hammers, safety glasses, and rakes. Their play became a child-size interpretation of our adult activities. While Brian worked on our house, the kids built structures out of extra pieces of two by four. While I sheet mulched the new garden, they used their rakes to move the straw out of the bed (sigh!). Every so often I find one of them sitting down with their hammer and a pile of nails to create something wooden. Usually this has no particular shape or purpose, but it's just the process of creating that is fun.

Perhaps this is the greatest lesson I learn from my kids—to enjoy the process, and not be so focused on the product. Homesteaders can be very product-centered. There is always something to be done—a fence to fix, a garden to plant, preserves to make. My favorite moments are the ones in which I can lose myself

in the process. The kids have taught me to slow down and smell the proverbial roses. To take time to check out every caterpillar, to peer into the mud living room of the five thousandth fairy house and truly see the small difference in the way the stick ladder was created, or to look closely enough at the chickens that I can maybe, just maybe, finally understand how to tell Cinnamon apart from Pumpkin.

Homestead Family Profile: Elisa Rathje
Salt Spring Island, British Columbia, Canada

Kids ages seventeen and twelve

Photo Credit: Erika Rathje

Q: How are your children a part of your homestead life?
A: For us, homesteading as a way of living came on slowly over the course of years. The more I learned, the more I wanted to learn, alongside the children, and with mentors in the farming community or just consulting good books.

Our children have always homeschooled and now they learn largely immersed in the homestead and the island community beyond it. They want to

---

be involved in nearly all aspects of its function and converse with us at length. They have opinions and growing experience supported by our encounters with folks in the community, farmers, artists, gardeners, orchardists, and permaculturists. I tell them about what I'm reading and they run with the ideas. We are all apt to research a new project deeply before we step forward, finding mentors, books, images, sites, and old resources. We debate the ethics of various decisions. When it occurs without coercion they are delighted to join in to tend the creatures or get the harvest in, and share thoughts about whether to preserve by drying, pressing, saucing, jamming, freezing, or cold storage.

Q: How are your children involved with your farmstead business?
A: They've been contributing to the homestead economy by harvesting for the farm stand, keeping poultry for eggs, and helping broody hens to raise broilers or layers. They plan their own small businesses within the farmstead: growing flowers, illustrating rural life for coloring pages, and selling crafts from the homestead at the farmers' market.

I chat with the girls about their work daily, hearing how the creatures are doing. We keep a chalkboard with tasks checked off so that we know fresh water or bedding has been seen to, eggs are tracked. I pitch in and can make adjustments like repairs, and my sweetheart and I make sure that we're well stocked with bedding and feed. We all manage the farm stand together. I'm leading, but they are responsible in themselves, and communicate well.

Q: How do you find balance between family, work, and homestead life?
A: Balancing family life, work life, homestead life—for me, the boundaries between these merged a long time ago. As an artist, much of my creative time looks very much like homesteading, or homeschooling. I manage best by using strong foundational routines that build in maintenance for our critical tasks. These are tracked in my planner and on a family chalkboard. We all prefer to keep our schedule incredibly open, aside from the daily chores. My sweetheart works from home, or travels, and our flexibility allows us to flow with whatever's next.

We focus on making more of what we need ourselves, at home, which leaves us great flexibility to meet with a mentor, do a workshop, take up a seasonal activity like horseback riding lessons or beekeeping visits, attend community events on the island, and host guests (our guests enjoy joining in on the farm!). I began rising early to give myself time to practice yoga, writing, drawing quietly in solitude. Much of our fun looks like a creative life at home, with tons of reading, making stuff, or getting out for a swim in the lake or a hike to the beach.

"My biggest challenge is remembering to include the children, rather than to do it all by myself. To empower them through involvement in anything I'm doing. It can take longer, and involve more discussions, more patience, staying open to the way they learn, and how much help they want, but now that they are older, I recognize that the family's involvement really does allow me to do so much more than I could ever do alone." —Elisa Rathje, Appleturnover.tv

CHAPTER ELEVEN: CLOSING THOUGHTS

If it seems that my style of homesteading with children is simply involving the entire family in the quiet routines of everyday life, then you are decidedly right! Homesteading is one important way to create a life that is in harmony with the rhythm of nature, an opportunity for our family to grow and raise food that we feel good about and that makes us feel good, and a way to explore the world around us by digging our hands into the earth and learning through hard work and experience.

Some of the memories that I will forever carry with me are the stark, beautiful homesteading miracles I've witnessed. The morning that Brian walked back from the pasture and told us, "There's a baby cow in the pasture." The time I was driving up the highway to meet my graduate school adviser, then promptly turned around because I decided that being present with Ella for her first baby goat birth was more important. The hours of ice skating on our homestead pond under a glorious blue winter sky, walking through the bare-branched woods with the kids to collect sap, and the sun-sweetened taste of the very first peach we harvested from our own tree.

Whatever your homesteading journey—whether you are brand-new to the adventure, or you've been on the path for years—folding your children into the joy, hard work, sadness, loss, and abundance of homesteading will never be anything but rewarding. Even if your kids decide that they hate homesteading and want to live in the city (as I've been told once or twice), the self-sufficient lessons of homesteading and the time your family has spent together will always remain.

Additional Resources

General homesteading resources:
The Nourishing Homestead by Ben Hewitt
The Weekend Homesteader by Anna Hess
Homegrown & Handmade: A Practical Guide to More Self-reliant Living by Deborah Niemann
My website, Homestead Honey: https://homestead-honey.com

Chapter Two: In the Family Kitchen
National Center for Home Food Preservation, an excellent resource for canning and other methods of food preservation: http://nchfp.uga.edu/index.html

Chapter Three: Foraging
Incredible Wild Edible, *The Forager's Harvest*, and *Nature's Garden* by Samuel Thayer
The Sugarmaker's Companion by Michael Farrell
Three ways to cold leach acorns: http://www.backyardforager.com/cold-leaching-acorns-three-ways/

Chapter Four: Family-Friendly Ferments
Wild Fermentation and *The Art of Fermentation* by Sandor Elix Katz
Traditionally Fermented Foods by Shannon Stonger
Sandor Katz's Wild Fermentation: www.wildfermentation.com
GEM Cultures: http://www.gemcultures.com/
Cultures for Health: http://www.culturesforhealth.com/
Ginger ale recipe: https://learningandyearning.com/ginger-ale/

Chapter Five: Gardening with Children
Farmer Boy by Laura Ingalls Wilder
The Resilient Gardener by Carol Deppe
Four-Season Harvest by Eliot Coleman
How to Grow More Vegetables by John Jeavons

The Suburban Microfarm by Amy Stross

Roots, Shoots, Buckets & Boots: Gardening Together with Children by Sharon Lovejoy

Kid-size gardening tools from Montessori Services: https://www.montessoriservices.com/primary-garden-tools

Adaptive Seeds: https://www.adaptiveseeds.com

Territorial Seed Company: http://www.territorialseed.com/

Baker Creek Heirloom Seeds: https://www.rareseeds.com

High Mowing Seeds: https://www.highmowingseeds.com

More information about seed balls and how they make a difference: https://seed-balls.com

Dill's Atlantic Giant Pumpkin Seeds, Park Seeds: https://parkseed.com/dills-atlantic-giant-pumpkin-seeds/p/05702/

Composting for the Homeowner, University of Illinois Extension: https://web.extension.illinois.edu/homecompost/default.cfm

Family Food Garden: https://www.familyfoodgarden.com

Uncle Jim's Worm Farm (source of red wiggler worms): https://unclejimswormfarm.com

More tips for making a two-bin worm composting system: https://www.tenthacrefarm.com/2015/01/the-lazy-gardeners-way-to-make-fertilizer/ and

http://working-worms.com/how-to-make-your-own-worm-farm/

Chapter Six: Caring for Animals

The "Living with" Series, *Living with Chickens* by Jay Rossier, *Living with Sheep* by Chuck Wooster, and *Living with Goats* by Margaret Hathaway, provides great overview of the care of each creature, without getting too technical.

A Kid's Guide to Keeping Chickens by Melissa Caughey

Hobby Farms: Rabbits: Small-Scale Rabbit Keeping by Chris McLaughlin

Chickens: Tending a Small-Scale Flock by Sue Weaver

The Small-Scale Poultry Flock by Harvey Ussery

Farm Anatomy by Julia Rothman

Our Animal Friends at Maple Hill Farm by Alice Provensen and Martin Provensen (This is a children's picture book, but one of my favorites!)

Margarita and the Beautiful Gifts by Janet Garman (Another children's book, which blends information about caring for ducks with a sweet story.)

Chickens for Backyards hatchery: http://www.chickensforbackyards.com

Meyer Hatchery: https://www.meyerhatchery.com

Chapter Seven: Preparedness

Opinel No 6 pocketknife: https://www.opinel-usa.com

72-Hour Kit Checklist: https://momwithaprep.com/72-hour-kit/

Federal Emergency Management Agency (FEMA): https://www.fema.gov

Ready campaign with information about preparing for, responding to, and mitigating emergencies: Ready.gov

Chapter Eight: Herbal Wellness

A Kid's Herb Book by Lesley Tierra

Rosemary Gladstar's Family Herbal by Rosemary Gladstar

Mountain Rose Herbs: https://www.mountainroseherbs.com/

Bulk Herb Store: https://www.bulkherbstore.com/

Chapter Nine: Handmade Homestead Crafts

Wild Color: The Complete Guide to Making and Using Natural Dyes by Jenny Dean

A Garden to Dye For by Chris McLaughlin

The Beeswax Workshop by Christine Dalziel

Acknowledgments

The seeds of this book were planted years ago but it has taken a collection of people to bring it to fruition.

Athena Williams gave insightful feedback that helped me flesh out an idea and turn it into an actual book proposal. Homestead Honey readers inspire me every day to dig deeper into homesteading and keep writing!

Thank you to Skyhorse Publishing and particularly to Abigail Gehring, for her guidance throughout this process. I feel fortunate to have such an inspirational writer and homesteader as my editor.

The SAH ladies are a source of daily encouragement, practical support, and infinite wisdom. I am so glad I get to spend virtual time with such a smart and sassy group of business owners and homesteaders. Special thanks to Janet Garman, Kathie Lapcevic, Kris Bordessa, Colleen Codekas, and Jan Berry for their extra doses of encouragement.

Thank you to Amy Stross, Kathie Lapcevic, Maya Wells, and Isis Loran for the use of their gorgeous photos.

Special thanks to Corina Sahlin, Devon Young, Shannon Stonger, Isis Loran, DaNelle Wolford, Ashley Browning, Justin and Rebekah Rhodes, Tessa Zundel, Lisa Bedford, Rachel Jepson Wolf, Angi Schneider, and Elisa Rathje for sharing your beautiful stories of homesteading with your children. And to Ben Hewitt for sharing the beauty in the ordinary through your words.

Huge thanks and love to our families, who have supported us on this sometimes crazy homesteading journey. And most importantly, I want to acknowledge my husband Brian, who is the most talented, kind, hardworking person I've ever met, and my children, Ella and Everett, who amaze me every day with their curiosity, intelligence, and creativity, and who posed for photos without (much) complaint. I love you all!

INDEX

ABOUT THE AUTHOR

Teri Page is the creator of the popular homesteading blog Homestead Honey and author of *Creating Your Off-Grid Homestead*. Born in the suburbs of Boston, Teri began gardening and homesteading twenty years ago, and her fingernails have been covered in dirt since!

A lifelong educator, Teri has taught marine biology, dance, musical theater, yoga, and gardening to kids of all ages. She is passionate about involving children in the daily work of homesteading as a way to deepen relationships and build self-sufficiency skills.

In addition to her passion for gardening, off-the-grid living, food preservation, and more, Teri is a life and business coach who works with women ready to live their homesteading dream.

You can learn more about Teri and access Family Homesteading bonus materials at www.familyhomesteadingbook.com.